TWO MOMS
AND A DAD

For my family, wonderful weirdos all.

TWO MUMS AND A DAD

TOBY ROBERTS

bad apple press

Two Mums and a Dad

First published in 2021 in Australia and New Zealand by Bad Apple Press, Pty Ltd, ABN 62 630 105 065, Sydney and Perth.

21   8 7 6 5 4 3 2 1

 A catalogue record for this book is available from the National Library of Australia

Edited by Karen Gee
Editorial assistance by Teaspoon Consulting
Text typeset and cover design by Bad Apple Press
Cover design by Bad Apple Press
Printed by Ovato Press

The paper used to produce this book is a natural, recyclable product made from wood grown in sustainable plantation forests. The manufacturing processes conform to the environmental regulations in the country of origin.

Author note: Some names have been changed, some events truncated and some peripheral characters merged, in order to give people plausible deniability.

Bad Apple Press titles can be purchased at **www.badapplepress.com.au**

CONTENTS

PART 1

MUM AND DAD

THE FiRST SiGNS

It was clear that Mum liked girls well before she left my dad. I'd just misread the signs.

When I was seven years old, Mum took me to meet her Year 12 students at the girls' school where she taught French. She sat me on a pile of books and two smiling teenagers cooed over my blond hair, leaving me with the mistaken impression that they loved me. They really loved my mum.

And there was a lot to love about Mum. She had perfect white skin and elfin features. The only thing that stopped her looking girlish was the severe helmet fringe she'd adopted in honour of the 1970s folk singers whose anti-establishment message she embraced so enthusiastically. Her free-spirited approach to teaching kids was fun too. A book called *The Children on the Hill* had convinced her that an environment of creativity and experimentation would yield bold and gifted children. While we all loved the plays and books and word games, her eccentricity must have been embarrassing for some people. I was too young to feel anything other than adoration, but to others it was clear that Mum was different.

Within a year of finishing school, both of those French students were living at our place in Beecroft (one of the duller suburbs of northern Sydney). Our three-level house could happily fit Juliet and Kelly, and Dad didn't seem to mind. He even described them as 'angels', though Mum knew they were naughtier than that. I don't think there was a sexual relationship underway between Mum, Juliet or Kelly at this stage, but it was clearly on their minds, judging by all the flirting and cuddles.

In the 1970s there was a general air of permissiveness when it came to bad fashion and sex. Underdressing was common around our house, but clothes became entirely optional on the first boat trip with the girls. Dad had just bought an oversized clipper, a captain's hat and a pair of fetching 'Miss Daisy' denim shorts to go with it. When your radiological practice is making too much money, one response is to buy a large boat and play dress-ups.

Dad performed the part of admiral with conviction – he was a tall man, proud and loud, well used to getting his way. But the effect was partly undone when he tried to stride the top deck with denim shorts wedged in his bum crack. If he kept still, he could convey the impression of an experienced seaman, albeit one who knew enough about real sailing to avoid the ocean altogether and stick to the Hawkesbury River.

We set out from Akuna Bay with Dad at the helm, my older brother Mark trying to make sense of his orders, my sister Ren already set up below deck with a board game, Mum and her two new friends up the top with the wind in their hair.

Ancient walls of forest rose at a dizzying incline on either side of the river, and crooked gums clung sideways to the rocks as if they were trying to get away from something. But I was more interested in the sight of Kelly and Juliet. Those two brunettes, so cherubic and lively, had brought a whole new air of excitement to our family dynamic.

A pristine cove opened before us and Dad commanded us to weigh anchor. I asked what that meant. Mark seemed to know, so the rest of us piled into the rowboat and headed for the beach. Somewhere between rock hopping, sand writing and oyster prying, Kelly and Juliet's clothes fell off. I don't remember questioning how or why that happened; I was too shocked by the luxuriance of their pubic hair, which was wilder than the scrub around us. It suddenly occurred to me that Dad was growing something similar on his face – his red beard nodded approvingly at us from the top deck of the boat. Grooming had been abandoned along with good judgment.

That night, the adults had their pants back on, Dad drank wine and Mum held court with her two adoring protégés. Even if Dad wasn't getting any direct action, he seemed happy enough. I imagine he thought of himself as some kind of Norman Lindsay, orchestrating naked romps in the bush with sylvan beauties drawn by his charm. In any event, jealousy was dismissed as an unhelpful emotion in our family, and I'm guessing Dad was free to take his pleasure where he found it.

After dinner, the tinkle of the wires on our mast and the slap of the water against the fibreglass hull had me halfway into a dream when Dad's voice frightened me back to the world. 'Toby, come up and play something.' I'd taken up the violin a few years before and it was now as much a part of my identity as white hair and heron legs. I didn't mind playing the fiddle, but others seemed to get more of a kick from watching me. The upper deck fell under a reverent hush as I set up my stand and music.

I had learnt to detach myself at performance time and play without nerves, though the price for that level of remove was a certain emotional blankness. That night I was more attuned to the navy-blue air than the Boccherini ringing from the sound hole under my ear. I was like a monkey playing cards without any understanding of the game, and my left hand felt possessed as it skipped nimbly over the finger board.

Mum and Dad watched on with pride, and Juliet nodded along politely, but Kelly was transfixed. When my last note faded and the gentle aquatic sounds reclaimed the night, Kelly said breathlessly, 'I'm learning the viola. I can't wait to play with you.'

Back home in Beecroft, music drew me and Kelly closer together. I practised hard, and Mum's supervision took on an obsessive quality (Mark and Ren were harder to teach, perhaps having absorbed her message about independence too well).

Kelly and I began playing duets, her deeper resonant strings underpinning my melodic passages like a darker layer of chocolate below cream. She always complimented me on my playing so I decided she must be very wise as well as pretty.

Juliet's sleepier charm was working its way into my heart as well. She took it in turns with Mum to read me bedtime stories, and I looked forward to those sessions, when her steady cadence would draw me down to sleep and her brown eyes seemed to swim beneath her glasses like some gentle sea creature. To have three supportive women in my life seemed an impossible blessing, but after a time it became clear, even to me, that a strained competitive tension was developing between Juliet and Kelly.

Kelly was the more beautiful of two, with a wild gypsy flash to her dark eyes, and a musical voice. I think she was also brighter, as my mother seemed astonished at the speed with which she adopted a new language; but like so many smart young things her talents must have come with a bundle of neuroses, which made her difficult at times. Mum certainly seemed more in control with Juliet, and perhaps Kelly's volatility looked less attractive when set against Juliet's placid, steadfast nature.

My father's place in the family dynamic was changing too. What must have seemed a male fantasy at first – a clutch of nubile young women under his roof – probably lost its gloss once it became clear that he was not the centre of gravity. I imagine he felt destabilised by the emotional ties that had blossomed so quickly between Mum and her girlfriends, though I never credited him with those feelings at the time. He built a study out by the garage, which I thought was a cunning strategy to keep us out, though perhaps *he* felt excluded, drifting further from Mum's emotional orbit.

From their earliest days at university, Dad had been the boss. Mum had willingly deferred to the confident older boy on all matters, but now with Kelly and Juliet she got to play the wise elder, and I think she liked it.

Around this time Mum fell pregnant with my little brother. Years later, Dad confided that he was at least partly motivated to have another child by a desire to draw the family closer, though deep down he must have known that a screaming ball of vomit would do no such thing. Mum was experiencing growing pains of every sort, and our family fabric stretched along with her tummy. The hormones from her pregnancy caused her teeth to move so much that one of them cracked. The only solution at that time was a full set of medieval braces.

She also chose that moment to resign from her teaching position and begin studying for a Masters in Psychology. In addition to a mouth full of barbed wire, she was managing a fiery husband, two live-in lovers, an adolescent daughter who liked slamming doors, and two boys who were unhappy at school.

2

JULiET WiNS OUT

Knowing there was another sibling on the way made me unhappy – I was used to getting most of the attention and didn't want that to change. But school was making me miserable too. Beecroft Primary was all drab asphalt, with buildings like scout halls. You could tell the teachers were bored with teaching, and the students felt the same way. Even playtime was mechanical: kids patted tennis balls back and forth across a painted line with their mouths half open. The only ritual that held any real interest was a bizarre one – bum sniffing.

Older kids sought relief from the monotony of the place by sticking their heads over the toilet partition in order to tease the pooers below. As a result, some children avoided the toilet, preferring to hold it in until they crapped themselves. Rather than turn on the older boys who started it all, Year 3 students hunted the victims, developing a foolproof method for finding them: lining everyone up at the end of lunch to sniff their backsides. Kids in grey shorts took their place facing the wall, like inmates awaiting a prison camp execution.

Mrs Lambert was my Year 3 teacher. Mum kept a school report from her which referred to me as scholastically challenged but helpful with cleaning up. The tone of it suggested I might be retarded. She seemed to loom enormous and unyielding, with steel-wool hair, but I saw her on a train station about ten years later and nearly laughed. She'd been replaced by a benign little dwarf who looked like she needed a cuddle.

At the time, though, it was me who needed the cuddle. On the day I learnt about Mum's pregnancy, I sat on the steps outside my classroom with John Fidelis. I asked if I could have one of his Twisties. He began grinding them into powder within the packet in order to make that impossible.

I wasn't easily deterred.

'Can I have some?'

'Nah, I'm savin' 'em,' he said.

That was a fair excuse at the time. The idea that you'd prefer to mutilate your Twisties and eat them rubbery stale rather than share them with your friends was well accepted at Beecroft Public.

I came home that afternoon and told Mum that I wasn't going to school any more. 'All right darling, we'll find you another school,' said Mum, which wasn't quite the outcome I'd planned. I would have preferred no school at all. 'Anyway, we have to get you to swimming lessons now,' she added. 'Let's talk about it later.' I hated swimming almost as much as I hated school, and I cried to get out of both, but it was no use – my sister was going to training and I was going too.

At twelve years of age, Ren was already close to her full impressive height, and still learning to occupy that frame. She had fair hair, soft blue eyes and a serious set of shoulders courtesy of the laps she was banging out every afternoon in the swimming pool. I dunked my head in the fetid water of the pool, still brooding about the need to attend school and wondering if it might be easier to drown. Evidently the teachers thought I might do that by accident, because my demonstration lap in the junior squad ended with me dangerously close to the bottom of the pool. One of the supervisors came to the edge of the water to ask if I was okay. I tried to reassure him that this was just the way I swam (a sort of downward motion, using the bottom for propulsion) but water filled my mouth when I opened it to speak. Once out of the pool I could see Ren joking with her fellow squad members and pretending we were unrelated.

When we arrived home, we found Kelly going through the family photos in the lounge room: Dad the golden boy holding his medical degree like a sceptre; Dad and Mum at dinner, his face now heavy with authority, hers like an Audrey Hepburn doppelganger; and another one of Mum in her semi-professional ballet days, looking perfectly balanced and delicate. 'You didn't tell me you danced!' Kelly scolded Mum.

Mum seemed proud and embarrassed. 'Do something for me,' Kelly pressed.

Mum put down our swimming bags and spun lightly on the spot. 'Wow!' we all clapped. Ren knew how to get a laugh and saw an opportunity to coax one from Kelly, her new idol. (A few years earlier, Mum had urged Ren to take up ballet in the hope it might spark the same creative fire it had kindled under her, but it didn't spark anything other than an instinct for parody.) Ren launched into her signature piss-take move – a slight cock of the hips to make an arabesque look like a dog taking a slash. 'Do it again,' Kelly laughed in delight.

The next weekend I had my opportunity to impress Kelly. Mum had encouraged us both to try out for the Sydney Youth Orchestra and auditions were held at the Conservatorium on a steamy summer's day. Kelly was so nervous she took beta blockers to get through the ordeal, while I played my set pieces with at least half a mind devoted to lunch. Our moods reversed the following weekend when Kelly learnt that she'd been accepted into the orchestra for 18-to-24-year-olds, and I found out I was in the orchestra for little ones, a long way from the comfort of Kelly's presence.

In my first orchestral rehearsal we all started together but shifted by degrees, moving on at slightly different speeds until eventually we were producing very modern sounds that the composer had never envisaged. In the years to come, I would play with orchestras that felt like a plane taking off, all parts firing in concert, a colossal wave of sound pouring from the back. At this stage, though, it was more like a shopping cart listing down a hill.

Our conductor had wispy clown hair and an overbite. He was muttering 'Yum fuddy duddy duddy' to mark the semi-quavers, working in ever more frantic and exaggerated motions to rein in the disaster. We continued to stare at the music, our short legs swinging off the ground, no thought for the conductor, intent only on finishing the piece. The piano accompanist played louder and louder, a 'stay with me' expression of panic stretched across her face.

Kelly and I compared notes on the way home. 'How was your group?' Kelly asked, panting with exhilaration. 'The air conditioning was nice and cool.' I felt it was important to say something positive.

My brother Mark was in Year 9 at an Anglican college where Dad was paying good money to have him properly prepared for life. Mark had already developed a small but profitable business renting the pornographic magazines he'd found under the house, and on-selling marijuana to younger boys at a steep mark-up, which was probably more practical commercial training than Dad had envisaged. By now, naughtiness was inducing a chemical reaction within him, even stronger than the drugs he was taking with ever-greater regularity.

He'd also mastered enough chords on the piano and guitar to mangle a tune, and duly formed a band, mainly to secure more attention from girls. That Sunday, family and friends got to hear their 'party setlist'. Mark and his friends set up a drum kit, plastic synthesiser and a guitar without an amp, while my father locked himself in the study.

The band played Adam and the Ants' 'Ant Music', which I only recognised because of the gel in their hair and the stripes painted on my brother's face. Actual music from ants would have made a greater impression on the small audience, who stared down at the grass on the front lawn and kept perfectly still in the hope that this would bring things to a close more quickly. The synth player stopped hitting his keyboard and struck an awkward pose – face straining to the heavens – which was our cue to clap. Mum congratulated them on their bravery, in much the same way that a streaker might be congratulated at the football.

The drummer, Peter, told me many years later that my brother was so buoyed by the performance he rushed to a laundry cupboard to find some cleaning agents to sniff. Peter tried telling him that whisky from my father's study might have a more reliable narcotic effect without some of the unpleasant side-effects associated with chemical solvents, but the talk didn't put Mark off. Most of this behaviour was just showing off, though some of it was genuine unhappiness.

Dad and Mark were not getting along. Mark had been getting into trouble at school for not applying his big brain, getting into trouble with the State Rail Authority for not following passenger protocol (like remaining in the carriage when the train is moving), and getting into trouble with the police for generally being a dickhead. Mum did her best to mediate between them, but she was managing conflict on a number of fronts – some subtle shift had unbalanced the triangle between her, Kelly and Juliet. I learnt, years later, that Kelly was undecided about her sexuality at this point. In any event, Juliet became the key confidant as Mum's pregnancy progressed.

Feeling the game turn inexorably in Juliet's favour, Kelly chose to retire from the field altogether. In the lead-up to our first SYO performance at Taronga Zoo, Kelly told me she was leaving Beecroft for a very old country where people ate pancakes and it snowed at Christmas time. I was sad for a full two hours, before Mum read me a story.

On the day of the performance, we travelled to the zoo without Kelly. When we arrived, a fierce wind was blowing and we had to attach our music to the stands with clothes pegs. Even with that precaution, our white sheets flapped horizontally like the wings of seagulls, and our chaotic, dissonant sounds swirled off in little eddies towards the surrounding bushland. The noise of immigrant parents (grumbling in Russian, Hebrew and Mandarin about the decision to place a children's orchestra in a forest) somehow came more clearly to my ears than the instruments of my fellow musicians. But when it was over, they all stood and cheered as if we'd defeated fascism.

As a reward for me finishing within a few seconds of everyone else in the orchestra, Mum allowed me to ride home with Juliet. This was a special treat because she had a Holden Torana with a leather gearbox, and I was allowed to put it into first gear at the traffic lights. She also had a stereo that played Elton John and 10cc, rather than Beethoven and Bob Dylan. She smiled at my look of wonder.

'Did you like the concert?' I felt emboldened to ask.

'It sounded beautiful,' Juliet lied kindly.

As we drove home, I stole sideways looks at her gentle bovine face. I was adjusting to the new regime already but the family mood had clearly changed.

Into this tempestuous world, baby Josh arrived with an enormous head, presenting yet another challenge for my mother. In the preceding days, I'd asked earnestly if the baby came out the bum hole, and Mum may have actually wished it did. From the very start, I was fascinated and repulsed by my little brother. Holding this fragile package was an awesome responsibility, but the crying grated on my nerves like a siren and changing his nappies revealed a vile slush. He wasn't a cute 'tissue ad' baby: his head was disproportionately large – he couldn't even touch his hands above it, but it was funny watching him try, flapping those little T-rex arms so ineffectually.

He graduated quickly from a rocking bassinette to a seated device with wheels and a harness that allowed him to paddle around on our wooden floors like the Daleks I'd seen on *Doctor Who*. Soon he could whir into the kitchen with surprising speed, his giant head flopping to one side from the momentum. Mum's greatest fear was that the gate to the stairs would be left open and he would hurtle down them, trapped inside his walking device. I was less worried about that. Josh had already begun to irritate me. Juliet was essentially joint carer for Josh, taking on a huge amount of the work, but Mum was still with him more often than me. A psychologist would no doubt explain my growing animosity towards Josh by pointing out that a child like me, who had enjoyed ten years of adoration as the youngest of three, might now feel supplanted. And there is probably some truth in that, but I prefer to think that he was just an annoying little cunt.

Even before Josh was verbal, we wound each other up like two cartoon adversaries, cycling back to the same position at the start of each new day. I had more subtle arts at my disposal, but he learnt soon enough that crying brought blame my way. I can't deny that I tormented him terribly. I can only say that he boxed above his weight when it came to retaliation. For all that, I was shattered when he did finally drive his walking device down the stairs, clipping his big squishy skull against every wooden edge on the way down. The crashing, wailing catastrophe echoed throughout the house and I dropped to the ground in despair, mostly at the thought that I would be in trouble for leaving the gate open. Turns out it was my sister who had left it open. Josh was rushed to hospital.

While we all waited for news from the hospital, Juliet started to cry. With so much stress and mothering responsibility on her young shoulders, it was easy for us to forget that she was only 20 years old. A few hours later we learnt that Josh hadn't suffered any lasting damage, but the strain of the event affected everyone, including me. The night after Joshy's accident, shocked into a new understanding of mortality, I cried outside Mark's door, devastated at the thought that Mum and Dad would eventually die. I'm not sure why I didn't go the extra step and start worrying about my own death, but Mark mustered up some sympathy and led me into his dimly lit room.

'What's wrong Tobes?' he asked.

'Mum and Dad are going to die,' I sobbed.

'Yeah. That's bad. Here, listen to this.'

Mark pressed a button on his exciting new digital watch and it began to play 'The Yellow Rose of Texas' in a metallic shriek. He held up his watch to a microphone on his lower bunk and tweaked a series of leads. A small set of speakers, which he'd salvaged from the local garbage tip and nailed to each cornice in the ceiling, took up the awful, repetitive jingle. Amplification made the song even worse but I didn't care – this was innovation, and my brother might as well have been Dick Tracy.

Only Dick Tracy was now frowning at one silent speaker above his top bunk. He climbed onto the IKEA safety rail to reach the offending area and reached behind the connection point. There was a sound like a mosquito being zapped. Mark said 'Ah, fuck' and the song suddenly rang from every corner of the room. Mark nodded his head in time to the tinny sound, and I left his room no longer caring that we were all going to die.

Around this time, I received the first of a number of cards from Kelly and a new friend of hers called Simon. They appeared to be travelling around the world. As the winter of 1982 approached, we learnt that Kelly was coming home. 'Kelly is dropping around this afternoon,' Mum told us excitedly after getting off the phone. 'Is she back for good?' asked Ren, hopping from one giraffe leg to the other. 'I think so,' said Mum. She looked to me for a reaction. I was more interested in Juliet, who wore a tight smile. Did reconnecting with an old school friend outweigh the renewal of a turf war?

The visiting hour approached and we had to take our growing restlessness outside. Mum, Ren and Juliet lined up at the bottom of the driveway like a royal reception committee. The presence of an audience always thrust Mark into performance mode, even if he wasn't supposed to be the star. He grabbed his skateboard and ran to the top of the driveway. Our place had a long battle-axe driveway, with a savage bend at the end which had brought many of us unstuck over the years. But in the right conditions, Mark could go all the way down, standing up. Today was one of those days, and he worked the bend in a magnificent sweep, the wheels on his board roaring to a crescendo as they crunched the uneven bitumen. His wiry frame formed an acute angle with the hill, like a sailor leaning out of his boat in a gale.

Mum and Ren were only faintly interested in Evel Knievel but I was awestruck, jealous and goaded into action. I climbed the steep drive feeling determined but also curiously condemned. At the top, I could look down on our sprawling yellow house and the valley below. In my lonely self-imposed hell, I desperately wanted to be back in the warm embrace of the kitchen, but there was nothing for it now – I had made it all the way down without an audience just the week before, and now was the time to prove it.

The presence of nerves made me reluctant to work the arcs from side to side, which meant I gathered too much speed from the start. Even the rumble of the wheel trucks, too loud at only a third of the way down, screamed their warning. The yapping little dogs on our eastern fence agreed. They ran the wire barrier in eager anticipation of blood, and got their wish well before the driveway bend. The death wobbles took hold quickly and expanded with the inevitability of ripples across a pond. The transition from air to gravel is always abrupt. The breath was knocked right out of me. Shock and humiliation had me crying before the pain set in. I tried to blubber with my head away from the crowd, but I had to keep looking back to pick the stones from my bleeding palms. Attention from the family, who now gathered around in a circle to commiserate, just made the tears come harder. 'Too fast at the top,' Mark concluded helpfully, giving me an awkward pat on the back.

Baby Josh decided to follow suit, despite the audience being too absorbed in the blood that was welling from my grazes to notice him push his ride some of the way up the hill. At 22 months, he was talking (mostly gibberish), walking and riding a plastic truck with pock-marked wheels. Preferring to ride nude, Josh had donned ug boots as a solitary concession to the autumn chill. Before I'd even made it to the carport, with nurses in attendance, Josh was away. His jowls wobbled in sympathy with the bumps, and his oversized head fought the centrifugal pull that threatened to drag him off balance as he turned the bend. But it was no use and he ended in the rose bush, where so many errant riders had come to rest before.

Now my mother had to contend with two crying sons and the real competition hadn't even begun yet. She rushed us through the front door and into the kitchen. Juliet pulled the leaves from Joshy's hair while Mum applied yellow iodine to my knees and hands. When I was coated in the ghastly stuff, Ren called 'Kelly's here!' from outside, where she'd stayed for the start of the real show.

Kelly came into the kitchen with Ren tagging shyly behind. 'Hello,' everyone called at once, burying Kelly in a series of hugs. She backed up from my hug to get a better look – 'Toby, my goodness, you're big!' I wasn't, but she was. All those Dutch pancakes had given her a full set of Rubenesque cheeks, and the northern clouds had robbed her of all colour, but she was a whirl of energy. 'And this must be Josh,' she said, patting the head of the boy who stared open-mouthed at all the hubbub, tears and snot still drying on his face.

'You're taller than me, Ren!' Kelly made it sound like an accusation. 'How is high school?'

'Okay,' said Ren, looking at her feet.

'Some of the girls are a bit mean,' Mum explained in response to Kelly's raised eyebrow.

'You have to meet my sister,' said Kelly encouragingly. 'She's in Year 7 too. She'll love you.'

My attention wandered, half-listening to Mum and Kelly talk about the Dutch, and watching Juliet who smiled a quiet smile from her kitchen chair. Sensing something grown-up was afoot, I retreated to the kitchen balcony, which soared above a riot of trees. The bush stretched all the way down our property and onto the park at the bottom of the hill. I held a small jar of raw sugar, which could lay out neat rows of granules on the hand railings if you tipped it correctly. Then I waited for the lorikeets to descend and fight one another. Mum and Kelly retreated to a quieter room, while I set about giving native birds gas and diabetes.

A while later, I saw Kelly give Mum a longer hug, before leaving us without saying goodbye. She appeared to have been crying. We saw less of Kelly after that and I never thought to ask why. Looking back, I think she was saddened to find things so settled without her and saw no obvious place for her to reclaim. Maybe she was filled with regret for having left in the first place. Mum may have simply told her it was over.

Kelly's withdrawal from our lives upset Mum badly because she could never abide being disliked.

Juliet seemed to grow in confidence once her position in the household was unchallenged and, by now, she and Mum were sleeping together. She was sufficiently embedded in our lives for Mum to invite Juliet's parents to breakfast. Mr and Mrs Fife came to our place the following weekend. They wore sensible eyeglasses like Juliet, and had round placid faces which, together with their sensible knitwear, reminded me of the Wombles. I stayed just long enough to eat my egg, only half-hearing Dad and Mr Fife talk about boats, before I went into the back garden to play with a wooden sword.

Many years later, Mum explained that the Fifes had received a number of shocks in the two years before that breakfast. They were good Christians from the northern suburbs, he did accounts while she dutifully tended to the home, and they were both very proud of their two children, who until recently had held leadership positions at their school and regularly attended church alongside their mum and dad.

All that had changed when news spread within their church community that Juliet's brother had debauched a fellow congregation member on the church grounds (entirely consensually). That scandal obviously caused the Fifes some acute social embarrassment, but it seemed to act as a kind of licence for Juliet. Her brother had blazed a trail with gelignite and now her homosexuality would seem tame by comparison. In other words, she had an excuse to stop attending church and start kissing girls.

Mum said Juliet's parents were very confronted by their daughter's sexual orientation but they never withdrew from her. Once they'd processed the shock, they were accepting of Juliet's choices and even affectionate towards Mum. After a while, their only real worries revolved around Juliet's physical safety when she went out with friends to see bands. It was one of many examples from my childhood where staid conservatives surprised everyone, including themselves, by ultimately embracing gay family members and friends.

A few weeks after the breakfast with Juliet's parents, the dust from Kelly's departure appeared to settle and the mood of the house lifted again. We were all set for our annual trip to the snow. Dad insisted on leaving in the middle of the night in order to avoid the traffic, so we were sent to bed early that Saturday night (though sleeping was impossible for any of us in that state of excitement). I emerged unrested to find the moon high and the Volvo packed, with a special seat reserved for me at the rear of the car, facing backwards, surrounded by mountains of luggage. It felt like a cubby house so I was ecstatic.

'Can I fill up at the Caltex, Dad? Can I do it?' Mark talked faster when he was excited.

'Don't put your feet on my bag,' said Ren.

'I've already done it,' Dad eventually answered, after double-checking the dashboard gauges.

'What about Goulburn?' Mark continued to press.

'Mum, tell Mark to keep his shoes on. His feet stink,' Ren continued to snipe.

'Quiet!' said Dad in the tone that always brought silence.

'Here,' Juliet whispered, taking Ren's bag from under Mark's feet and placing it on her own lap to avoid any further tension. This was a welcome development – a moderating influence that I could feel, even facing the wrong way.

We pulled out gently onto the empty streets of Beecroft and soon the only sound was the soft whistle of the Volvo's bulky shape fighting against the night air.

'Mum, can we play Duran Duran?' asked Ren, knowing the answer.

'Maybe later darling.'

Ren tapped a soft beat against the glass beside her, possibly 'Hungry Like the Wolf'.

'What's that sound?' Dad snapped, hyper-vigilance coming out as anger. Any flapping from the luggage on the roof raised the spectre of bags flying chaotically across a freeway. But in this case it was just the sound of a frustrated teen, and when Ren admitted as much, Dad nipped it in the bud. 'Stop it!'

When the streetlights of Sydney had given way to wooded darkness, Mum chose some music to cover the semi-audible hum of my father's nerves. Mum's tastes skewed toward Janis Ian, Bob Dylan and other folksy rubbish which indelibly shaped my ear, and in retrospect probably qualified as child abuse. On this occasion she chose Steeleye Span, a band that played electrified versions of English folk songs, often featuring grim snippets of medieval life, which appealed to the history-loving tastes of both my parents. Neither of them thought twice about the lyrical content, and we all sang along merrily to the tales of garrotted gypsies and murdered babies. It did the trick this time as well, luring Dad out of his fixed stare and back into quiet conversation with my mother.

'She really is very attractive,' Dad noted in relation to the lead singer. 'She could have been a model.' A man with a clearer sense of his own interests might have kept my mother's attention away from attractive ladies, but at least he was talking.

'I'm like the person who shoots the gun out the back of a spaceship,' I announced. I felt everyone should know.

'The rear gunner,' Mark clarified.

Ren's grumpiness had surrendered to sleep.

A truck rumbled alongside us and overtook with such a mighty whoosh of air that the Volvo shook for seconds afterwards. Dad muttered angrily. Some kind of challenge must have been issued between men of a certain disposition because we sped up and soon overtook the same truck.

Minutes passed, and my father was no longer talking. He could no doubt see in the rear view mirror the same thing I could see looming up behind us – a menacing castle of lights. The truck came within feet of our bumper bar. The driver's face was lost in the blaze of light, but his mood was obvious because he overtook again with a savage lurch.

Dad was already swearing before the truckie leant across his cabin, lowered the window on his passenger side and threw out an open can of beer that bounced off our bonnet and sprayed the windscreen in opaque froth. Dad hammered the brakes, the car tyres shrieked and the whole vehicle pulled to the left before coming to a stop in the gravel, several metres from the road. Dad was panting and everyone bar Josh was wide awake in shock.

'What was his number plate?' Dad shouted to Mum.

'He's mad!' Marko said approvingly.

Dad and Mum were both out of the car – one checking for damage, the other wiping down beer. Juliet soothed us down. 'It's okay. All over now,' she said reassuringly.

Within a few minutes, the purple had receded from Dad's face and we were underway again. No music or talking until Goulburn.

The holiday got better after that. Once free of the car and set up in the lodge, Dad chose to read by the fire while we tore down the mountains. In the evenings, sleeping arrangements weren't really discussed. I ended up with Mark, Ren ended up with Juliet and Josh, while Mum and Dad got the big bedroom. But Mum never seemed to go to bed at the same time as Dad. Either she stayed up with Juliet in the lounge room or retired early to read to us. I didn't give it a second's thought at the time, but the co-sleeping arrangements were exactly that – for sleep. It must have been a sad and lonely time for my father, feeling alienated from a wife he still adored, but all I gathered at the time was a vaguely unsettling feeling of tension.

3

CASUALiTiES

We came home the following week to find our guinea pig, Mr Gladstone (named for his prodigious sideburns, which made him look like the English prime minister of old), stiff and lifeless.

'How did he die?' wailed Ren. 'Did we do something wrong?'

'No, darling,' said Mum gently. 'It was very cold and maybe he died from that.'

'Isn't that what his fur is for?' Mark wasn't helping.

'Yes, but they're only small. You know, Juliet is bringing some friends around this afternoon,' Mum tried diverting us.

'Will we bury him?' sobbed Ren.

'Are they girls?' Mark was undeterred by the fact that all previous girls brought to the house were lesbians.

'Yes, darling. And yes.' Mum was beginning to resemble one of those table tennis maestros who can play two opponents at the same time. Luckily for her, I was too shocked by the first death in our family to make it a four-way contest.

'Can I make Mr Gladstone a little thing to go on his grave, you know, to remember him?' sniffled Ren.

'That would be lovely,' Mum agreed (though perhaps not as lovely as leaving Mr Gladstone enough food to last a week on his own).

'Won't Bodkin dig him up?' Mark frowned, thinking about our skittish Afghan dog.

'I don't think so, sweetheart.'

'Can we get another guinea pig?' asked Ren. Apparently she'd finished remembering Mr Gladstone.

'Maybe one with more fluff?' said Mark, having now accepted the unlikely cause of death.

'Of course,' Mum was relieved to escape further interrogation.

The hard work of grieving largely done, we began preparing to receive our guests.

The grind of childcare had been taking its toll on Juliet. Whenever she took off her glasses to wipe them clean, her exposed eyes had the look of sea creatures shucked from their shell. She must have felt prematurely thrust into middle age, so lately she'd begun to go out more often on the weekends, seeing a new set of friends in town, all of whom were bohemian, creative and homosexual. Juliet even joined a band with some of them, and had become especially tight with the saxophonist, Vicky Collard, who came to our house that afternoon, along with her younger brother Paul. They blew into our house like a storm front.

Something of Dad's stern nature lingered in the air of 154 Copeland Road, often making young people less confident and open. But the Collard family seemed immune to all that. Vicky shrieked and laughed with Juliet, embraced Mum like a long-lost sister and generally owned the kitchen. She looked and sounded like a cockatoo, with her piercing voice, prominent beak and orange plumage. Paul was just as theatrical. He encouraged me to give him 'five', then withdrew his hand before I could hit it, leaving me embarrassed and awestruck as he swaggered over to greet Mark. Soon the two older boys were ensconced in Mark's room with the door closed, while Vicky unpacked her saxophone in the lounge room.

Our lounge room held the most commanding position in the house. A full 10 metres wide, with glass overlooking the back garden, the lounge room housed antique music stands and a faux Renaissance chaise longue. I always felt a kind of pride at showing the room to newcomers. Vicky seemed undaunted by the space, and happily set up while talking to Mum about the kinds of music she liked. Mum took out her treble recorder, a large, dark wooden instrument which wouldn't have looked out of place at a medieval fair. Vicky took out her gleaming alto sax and suddenly Mum's tastes appeared more old-fashioned than quirky. After an excruciating search for a key signature that could accommodate both sax and recorder, which produced more semitone discords than a children's choir, they finally gave up and took it in turns to play their favourite pieces. Mum's Renaissance songs sounded hollow compared with Vicky's throaty rendition of the solo from 'Echo Beach'. Juliet looked on at her new friend with pride. Mum seemed somehow diminished.

As the weather warmed, we saw more of Vicky, and Vicky saw more of Mark than she'd intended. He'd recently taken up naturism, partly as a pick-up technique gone wrong, and partly as a deep-seated urge to challenge social norms. It served two purposes for Mark – he got to show off his dick and make people uncomfortable. On Vicky's second visit, Juliet was making her a cup of tea in the kitchen when Mark strode in naked and extended his hand to Vicky in greeting. The look on his face almost challenged the adults to reveal themselves as middle class and uptight. Vicky said 'Ooh' in surprise, but took her cue from the smiling room and shook Mark's hand without looking down. It was a neat recovery. The room was a tense blend of amusement and embarrassment, as Mum tried to steer the conversation onto music. Possibly disappointed at the lack of reaction, Mark sat up on the kitchen divider and cocked one leg wider for better effect, all the while agreeing casually that Ren's flute might be a better match for Vicky's saxophone than Mum's recorder had proved the previous week.

I could sense Mum's hand twitching for the Windex, wanting to wipe the counter when Mark got down to leave the room. She was caught in a cleft stick of her own creation, being such a fierce advocate of freedom of expression for children, though never envisaging that expression might take the form of bum cheeks being smeared all over the kitchen surfaces. It was the ultimate emperor's new clothes experience. But maybe she had the right approach because, a few months' later, Mark eventually got bored and stopped doing it. I don't remember anyone mentioning his nakedness at the time – nothing like, 'Oh, you're uncircumcised' or 'Fresh out, isn't it?'

At any rate, evidently the advertising paid off because one of Mum's old work colleagues invited Mark home a few days after seeing him nude and had sex with him. The achievement on his part was diminished by the fact that she was slightly mad and the pleasure of losing his virginity was dimmed by the venereal disease he contracted at the same time. Dad steered him off to a colleague for treatment, possibly proud as well as disgusted.

Vicky's brother, Paul, respected naturists and so became close friends with Mark, each amplifying the 'show off' in the other. Vicky brought out something childlike and fun in Juliet too. As often as Vicky came to our place, Juliet went out with her even more, so Mum did more with Josh, Dad spent more time in the study, and I was left to entertain myself. At the start of summer, a ferocious storm blackened the afternoon air, lightning branches fractured across the sky above the park, and the rain set in for days. Once the drum beat of the torrent settled into a steadier rhythm and the lightning strikes abated, I was allowed to walk to the park.

I emerged from the bottom level of the house wearing oversized gumboots and a hooded plastic coat. The expanse of bushland, running from our yard to the reserve, the creek and park, now blurred into one uninterrupted sprawl of green, all muted by the rain. Booth Park had a deep gully around its perimeter, precisely for days like this. The water frothed and boiled its way around the moat, pushing on to a stormwater drain. I stood in the broadest part of the stream, miraculously protected by my raincoat, twirling a stick through the milky currents around my legs. The air above me was strangely luminous and wonderful. When I finally came home, all that wonder evaporated in one sentence – 'Bodkin has run away.'

An enigmatic, slinking animal who was never particularly affectionate, Bodkin was nevertheless a treasured member of the household and we were all very worried. He hated storms and loud noises, and must have bolted at the first symphonic crash of thunder. We split into groups and scoured the neighbourhood. Ren and I walked the backstreets of Beecroft, including Cardinal Avenue, where we'd owned a house a few years earlier.

Ren led me down the uncurbed streets of the sheltered valley, still wet from the rain, pointing out features of our family's early life in hushed tones. Weed jungles grew up thick in the shade, and a creek ran through the yard of our old home, bearing frogs' eggs and twigs. I knew this simple square house intuitively and not at all. We'd moved out before I was five.

In between calling out for Bodkin, Ren relayed some stories I'd never heard before. She recalled Mum using cloth nappies on me, and being told that Dad had to be careful because he'd once stuck a pin through Mark's penis. I think this went some way to explaining the troubled love that grew between the two of them. Was it Freud's take on Oedipus that insisted boys lust after their mothers and fear their fathers' revenge through castration? Then on any analysis Marko had it tough – our mother was a porcelain beauty and Dad had tried to fashion him a new urethra. Dad was a young intern at the time but backyard surgery was not part of his training. I never learnt if there were lasting consequences and I was never brave enough to enquire because Mark only ever needed the faintest encouragement to whip the thing out.

As for Dad, the incident must have lifted his stress levels above their already substantial baseline. At an age when young men today are still living with their parents, my father was working brutally long hours at the hospital, paying off a mortgage, and mangling the penis of his first-born. To make matters worse, Cardinal Avenue crossed a road with blind corners, meaning accidents would sometimes bring Dad to the aid of shattered people in the middle of the night. Ren pointed out the black spot with a dramatic flourish.

I'm told Dad once attended a crash scene with a drunk driver that eventually wound up in court. A barrister discredited his evidence, mocking his 'wealth of experience' as an intern. I could just imagine my father's face glowing redder in the stand, his hands trembling with indignation at the attack on his authority. It soured him to legal proceedings forever. Aside from the heart-stopping scrape of tyres in the night, I gather the years at Cardinal Avenue were good ones. Mum and Dad were in love then, and Mark was a beautiful, open child.

As we walked back the way we'd come, Ren explained how much she'd looked up to my brother. A precocious walker and talker, Mark was keen to try anything and befriended strangers with his trusting heart. Dad didn't expect too much of him in those early years and he was allowed to grow free for a time. I remembered seeing footage of him, with a Beatle-esque mop of chocolate hair, doing stunts on the street where we stood now, working a crappy wooden skateboard from side to side when he can't have been much older than four. My momentary delight at that memory of Mark was touched with a hint of unplanned sadness. By degrees, that smiling Weet-Bix boy had become more haunted by his failure to please and by fear at home.

Ren and I returned home without seeing a trace of the dog. After many more days of trudging the neighbourhood streets and visiting local pounds, we eventually accepted the bitter truth that Bodkin was gone. As Christmas approached, family talk turned to a replacement dog, which should have been exciting, but I only felt uneasy. I wanted the changes to stop.

4

CHRiSTMAS CRiNGE

At least Christmas offered a set of defined rituals, unusual by the standards of other Australian households, but reassuringly normal for us. Having spent her childhood among German families in Galston, Mum had adopted their practice of celebrating with a feast at midnight on Christmas Eve. She'd also embraced the European traditions of communal carol singing, plays and other performances. At ten or even twelve years of age, I still found these things wildly exciting.

I was more than happy to take Mum's guidance on a performance, though Mark and Ren were quicker to resent her control. An uncomfortable dynamic was starting to emerge by this time – Mum wanting more from them, and the two of them wanting a longer leash. Fun stuff like family plays are only fun if you don't have to do them. The tyranny of being artistic on command is self-defeating. And perhaps Dad's embarrassment at eccentricity was starting to infect us too.

In the lead-up to the Christmas of 1982, we began

practising our four-part harmonies for the carols, and Dad jetted off to a medical conference in Bali. He promised to return before Christmas, bearing gifts from Asia, and said he was sorry to be missing the singing, though those last words didn't come out with any conviction.

Mum, Juliet and Vicky seemed less inhibited after Dad left, joking as we prepared the Christmas decorations in the lounge room. The last refinements to the Christmas tree made, Mum turned her attention to our singing parts. Soon we were heading up Copeland Road knocking on each door and performing unsolicited Christmas songs for the surprised occupants. This never struck me as odd at the time but I'm sure it perplexed our neighbours. Some kind of unspoken performance etiquette required them to stand politely through the whole ordeal, rather than call the police to have trespassers removed. If they'd known my older brother a little better, they would have had no hesitation in calling the police: in between singing his descant parts like an angel, Mark told me his plans for placing bungers and other explosives in their letterboxes.

On the morning of Christmas Eve, Dad returned from his conference looking refreshed and energised. He proudly produced some photos showing him 'at leisure' between professional sessions, wearing an enormous conical hat, white kaftan, bead necklace, red speedos and a pair of sandals. No doubt wanting to blend in with the locals, and knowing that oriental hats are set off to best effect atop the heads of large white men, I imagine he'd tried on various combinations before deciding that no pants were needed. But we were less worried about his dignity abroad and more worried about the things he'd brought back for us.

Dad didn't bother conforming with the family ritual of midnight presents and simply handed over the loot on the spot. We all got a set of intricately carved Balinese dolls, and stood spellbound, admiring their evil wooden faces. Dad rode a crest of family happiness, culminating in a lunchtime feast, where he held court at the head of our long wooden table. The size of our unusual family group meant Mum devoted a huge chunk of her life to meal preparation, and Christmas was the biggest exercise of the lot. In addition to the wave of courses, most big meals had a medieval theme, courtesy of Mum and Dad's obsession with all things historic, and none of us found anything incongruous about a king's feast being held within the confines of a 1960s yellow brick house whose brutal design would have happily passed inspection by a Soviet construction committee.

By early evening, Dad's enthusiasm for family time was waning. The furniture had been cleared from the lounge room to create a performance space and the first act was about to get underway. Mum's face was alight. Juliet and Vicky jumped up and launched into a stand-up routine while we all looked upward in awe from the carpeted floor where we sat. Mum laughed at the jokes so we did too. *The Women's Weekly* had just moved to a monthly publication cycle and Vicky pointed

out that the *Women's Monthly* had an earthier ring to it. That
got a cheer and I understood that some mysterious shift in
power was occurring even though gender politics was beyond
me. Vicky and Juliet both wore singlets without bras and
I could see tufts of hair under their arms. Dad was visibly
squirming.

The next act saw Paul wheel Mark into the room on Dad's
armchair. Mark craned his head to one side and raised a
clawed hand in a pretty convincing impersonation of a
child with cerebral palsy. Juliet and Vicky pretended to be
disgusted by-standers, wondering aloud why 'People like
that were allowed on the streets at Christmas time'. It was a
deadly earnest (and not especially sophisticated) exploration
of prejudice towards the disabled, but we all hailed it as
the greatest dramatic work since *Hamlet*. Mum hugged
Mark tightly afterwards, marvelling at his mimicry, borne of
close observation at some of Mum's fundraising events for
disabled youth.

I looked up to see if Dad shared my mother's appreciation
of Mark's performance but he'd returned to his study, the
cringe-inducing discomfort probably too much to bear. I
imagine he stood in his quiet space, without his chair, and
drank straight whisky from a tumbler. Mark wasn't far behind
him, celebrating his success with a cheeky glass of wine
which Mum tolerated as a Christmas indulgence. One glass
slid into four, and by the time we settled down to feasting,
Mark was drunk enough to lecture Ren on the meaning of *To*

Kill a Mockingbird, which she was studying that term.

'You have to understand the book in the content … I mean context, of American racing stations.' Mark regathered his tongue. 'Race elation. Race relations.' Ren's face wore a frown of impatience. The lapses in Mark's self-awareness steadily elongated to the point that he began reciting Monty Python's parrot skit and laughing at his own rendition.

I went to bed wondering what the new year would hold, with a brother and father so adrift.

5

OPEN REBELLiON

By early 1983, feminism had assumed a decidedly bolshie edge at 154 Copeland Road. Mum took to openly defying my father. On the afternoon of election day, my conservative father asked Mum who she'd voted for, knowing full well that he wasn't going to like the answer. Mum, surprisingly cool under fire, said 'It's a secret ballot darling.' We all froze.

'The last time those cretins were in power,' he said, referring to the Labor party, 'teachers nearly didn't get paid. Is that what you want? The country insolvent?' Dad was angry.

'It's my vote,' Mum countered breezily.

Rather than rage impotently in front of this audience, which was now listening intently, Dad stalked from the room, and time moved normally again.

Two days later, still processing the shock of a former union leader now running the country, Dad sat at the breakfast table trying to find articles in the paper that had nothing to do with Malcolm Fraser's defeat.

'That soldier bird,' he said, shaking the page with a picture of a young lady officer, 'was interviewed on the ABC last night.'

'Soldier bird, like the brown ones?' Ren asked innocently, not looking up from her cereal.

Mum sniggered at the misunderstanding, happy to poke fun at a sexist term. Dad's face reddened. Like a fart in church that becomes unbearably funny when you're not allowed to laugh, we were having trouble holding it in. Juliet sniggered, and soon the contagion was spreading.

'That's enough!' snapped Dad. Suppressed giggles continued to shake our shoulders until Dad put the paper down forcefully and marched from the room saying, 'I'm going to do the gardening. You might want to do something useful too.'

A guilty hush fell over us once he'd left.

When breakfast was over, we formed a conga line to wash, dry and return bowls. We were close to finishing up when a stricken cry ripped the air. It came from out the back and sounded like a man had been stabbed. Mark rushed to the verandah where he could look down on the backyard. 'Dad's hurt!' he said urgently and jumped over the balustrade, scaling effortlessly down the 3-metre pole which supported the verandah.

For the better part of two decades Dad had done no real physical exercise other than golf. Even his occasional games of squash had ended when his usual technique of occupying the middle space had resulted in a dislodged cornea from a ball to the face. All that inactivity came home to roost that morning. Moving a wheelbarrow load of bricks down our awkward back garden path, Dad had lost his footing and jarred his spine so badly trying to save the cargo that he ruptured several discs in his lower back.

Mark supported Dad with one arm draped over a shoulder, but even with that support Dad shuffled at a grotesque angle. His face was frighteningly pale. We all stood in shock as Mum helped him into the passenger seat of the Volvo and drove him off to hospital. I'd never seen Dad surrender the driver's seat.

My father's medical peers poked and prodded him before deciding that the best remedy would be to hack the dodgy discs from his back and fuse the remaining ones together. (These days, doctors would have told him to rest up then get to work on his mushy core, but that's much less interesting for the surgeons.) Dad came home hobbled and drugged, and was put to bed where he stayed for several weeks, only ringing a small bell from the bedroom when he needed attention. Once gingerly back on his feet, the key lesson he took from this whole painful episode was to never attempt any form of explosive activity again. The main lesson absorbed by the rest of us was this: the magnificent beast had fallen once, and it could happen again.

Maybe my brother was acting on these new signs of vulnerability, or perhaps he just wanted the old man's attention any way he could get it. In any event, Mark was getting wilder in his last year of school. First he got suspended for a stupid haircut (twin mohawks), then he crashed a car. He couldn't get that kind of attention from anything good he tried. In fact, trying at all became a hoodoo – you don't have to taste real failure if you have the excuse that you never put in the effort.

Solid as that logic sounds, the Higher School Certificate is not a handicap event, and no concession is made for the number of drugs ingested in the lead-up to the exams. Being a bright kid and ballsing up every test that year was one of Marko's stronger statements to Dad and the world.

As his early results in Year 12 began to indicate that universities would not be competing for his custom, Mum approached him about private tuition to supplement his school hours. Mark agreed in principle but argued that it needed the right kind of tutor. He nominated his drug-dealing friend Alistair, who had once sat a physics exam.

What Alistair lacked in knowledge he more than made up for with access to acid. So he and Mark embarked on a unique study regime consisting of LSD consumption and sleep deprivation. I'm sure this lent its own insight into the basic principles of movement, such as walking and how we often take it for granted, but curiously this did not translate into good grades for physics. (The funny thing about this is that to this day, Mark talks very knowledgably about physics, not at all daunted by the fact that he was off his head for the two short years he took the course in high school.)

To make things more embarrassing for Dad, Mark and his friends decided that they were punks, sharing (as they did) an affinity with the desperate working-class boys of London. I'm sure they never questioned the fit of the movement with their North Shore lives, and I certainly thought they were tough and terribly exciting. Mark had a girlfriend now too, which was even more exciting. Her name was Ghita, she was an exotic Italian beauty and her dad was an advertising executive who liked smoking pot.

Mark and Dad fought a lot that winter, mostly over Mark's behaviour and wardrobe, but the final fracture occurred over lawn mowing. Saturday mornings were always a flash point because Mark stayed up late and slept in, while Dad was an early riser no matter what he'd done the night before. Weighing up the risk of further spinal damage from our dangerously steep backyard, Dad delegated all mowing tasks to Mark, who demonstrated his enthusiasm for the task by snoring through any alarms or shouts that Dad directed his way. That winter, the frustrations had escalated on both sides to the point where Dad began running the lawn mower directly outside Mark's window, sometimes for a full 30 minutes, until either Mark had emerged angrily or the petrol in the mower ran out.

On the morning of their last big fight, the 'mower alarm' had done its trick, and Mark was heaving that clunky old machine up and down the uneven slope of the yard when he struck a piece of wood that flicked from the bottom of the blades and hit him above the eye. He ran to tell Dad that the job was becoming unsafe. Their shouts carried to the verandah where I crouched in dread and fascination.

'I'm not doing it any more. Look at this.' Mark angrily pointed at the cut on his face.

'Don't be ridiculous,' Dad said, vehemently denying any problem even as Mark's blood began to drip.

'*You* do it!' said Mark.

'Get back down there.' Dad's hand reached for Mark's shirt.

'Fuck you,' said Mark.

Dad drew back his other hand and held it, high and wobbling, through an awful period of indecision. Before the blow could fall, Mark shook himself free from Dad's grasp, ran up the side of the house, up the driveway and was gone. We didn't see him for days.

It took years for the lines of communication to fully open between them again. Even Mum had lost the ability to mediate their disputes.

A few months later, having bombed the HSC, Mark moved out of home and into Ghita's place. He didn't even say goodbye, and my sister struggled to forgive him for that. In her mind, theirs was an alliance that had seen them through the strangeness of childhood and he'd abandoned it without a second's thought. To be fair, I think he was more focused on saving his sanity than worrying about his siblings' feelings. If he'd asked, I would have told him my feelings of loss were mounting: first Bodkin, then Mark gone; Juliet half out the door, and Dad growing more troubled by the day.

6

THE COLLEGE

To make things trickier, this was also the year my parents sent me to private school. Over the prior two years, I'd been allowed to go to an alternative school in Dural called Narnia, which had no structured learning whatsoever, just hours of craft interspersed with playtime in the bush where we ran about and threw sticks at each other. It was the happiest time of my life. I guess naming a school after a make-believe kingdom should have been a clue, but my father was surprised by the fact that we didn't do sums.

At Narnia, kids were able to wear whatever they liked – usually kaftans made by hippie parents and sensible boots for stomping in the cow shit that filled the paddocks behind our classroom. I had my own alarming lapses in fashion judgment; there is a record of me wearing red velvet boots like something from an Errol Flynn movie. There's a point at which fashion risk strays into criminal negligence, and I'd found it. In my defence, I can only say parental guidance was sadly absent – one of them should have stripped the boots off me or considered adoption.

Guidance from teachers was also absent. Some of my favourite memories of Narnia involve breathtakingly irresponsible supervision. On some school excursions we were issued kerosene lamps, which we used in tents by ourselves. The school held cult-like ceremonies, encouraging us to send burning cardboard boats downstream and chant songs by the riverside to celebrate the turn of the seasons.

The teachers were often sleepy and confused, which made more sense to me later in high school when I took up smoking pot. The teachers also built the classrooms. There were tremendous hives of activity in some areas of the property, where wonderful hexagonal buildings would later emerge, all varnished to a gloss, with stained glass windows and colourful curtains.

Building work was so collaborative and communal it was almost Amish. No doubt the ceiling lights and other features were designed to map against the movement of the cosmos but probably did so at the expense of important load-bearing structures. A little scared at first, I soon embraced these things with a passion, although the thought of sitting in a room built by stoners, without an engineering degree between them, now fills me with horror.

We planted trees, told stories and staged our own plays in a wooden theatre. A lady called Ursula took us for 'eurythmy', where we were encouraged to feel the Earth's energy from the floor and imagine the ground speaking to us. I suspect Ursula may have dropped enough acid to actually hold a conversation with the floor but for the rest of us it was a little awkward.

I loved my teacher, Dave, so much that I took to calling Mum 'Dave', which I guess was a Freudian slip, given her comfort with trousers. In any event, it must have been difficult for Mum to answer to 'Dave' in public. But she would have accepted that impost in return for having me at a school with such impeccable hippie credentials. With all the dance, drama and painting going on in this bush school, I think she and Juliet secretly wanted to attend as well.

Throughout this time, I was dimly aware that I'd been booked into my older brother's uptight college for Year 6 but it seemed too distant to be real. Then suddenly it was all too real. The imprint of my miserable time at Beecroft Primary was still reasonably fresh, and the college was a monstrous version of the same thing: internal roads fit for a cavalcade, Roman colonnades, Dickensian buildings designed to dwarf your personality, and mighty ovals where boys stood in ranks like little soldiers. Here I would have to start again, just one of many frightened newcomers.

I think my parents had guessed, quite rightly, that I would not have withstood the shock of a transition directly into high school, nor would I have passed the entrance exam. Starting college in Year 6 neatly bypassed the academic assessment. There was just one test to determine the relevant competency level: in my case, C-stream. As Peter Cook said, 'They only asked me to write my name and I got 75 per cent for that.' In addition to spelling my own name, Mum drilled me tirelessly in times tables, grammar and the other fundamentals most children acquire naturally, provided their teachers don't ingest psychotropic mushrooms.

On my first day of school, George Weaver, a freckled charmer, told me that he would be my friend if I voted for him in the class elections. Some of the warmth of that connection dissipated as I watched him repeat the routine on every other new boy in the classroom. We elected him to office and, true to his word, he remained my friend for life, although I'm sure he's had cause to question that deal on a few occasions.

After an uncomfortable early period of tears and tussles in the playground, I formed a gang with George, Nate (a charismatic delinquent who reminded me of the Artful Dodger) and other assorted tough kids. From then on, the college held no fear for me. In those tiny neighbouring bodies I found the armour to shield against all assaults from other students and the oppressive might of the place itself. Though truth be told, there wasn't much oppression in the junior school, just a bunch of benign grandfatherly teachers who were occasionally exasperated but mostly bemused by my friends and me.

We believed our gang was only one step removed from the Bronx Warriors. We wagged school to travel to the city, prising apart the doors of our train in order to spit on the people waiting at the station. We stood uncertainly in alleyways looking for clues about how to conduct our gang lives, and only got a glimmer of insight on two occasions when skinheads robbed us of our tuckshop money. After those embarrassing episodes of wealth redistribution, we decided it was the lack of weapons that had really cost us. In future we'd carry iron bars and knives. Unfortunately, we couldn't find any so we had to make do with broken strips of hard plastic that could have caused a nasty scratch if we'd hit someone enough times.

The school became more irritated with us as our troublemaking confidence grew. Even gentle Mr Johnson, our regular teacher, began carrying a ruler to maintain silence during class time. He only used it on one occasion.

Educational studies no doubt endorsed singing exercises for the developing brain, but the song book *Let's Sing* didn't quite hit the mark. It featured a bunch of cringey folk songs from the 1970s with faux bush 'lingo' that even Henry Lawson would not have been able to recite without vomiting up his Scotch. Songs like 'Jake the Peg' lost their lustre by the second chorus, let alone their tenth reprisal. We'd all learnt to sing it while thinking about the petty acts of vandalism we'd commit on the way home, but one of the slower kids in our very slow class, Terry Andrews, hadn't learnt to disguise his boredom and was struggling to keep up the drone. Mr Johnston yelled and hit him so hard on the forehead with the ruler that the skin parted and blood pissed out. I'm not sure who was paler: Terry, who was losing his blood, or the teacher, who imagined losing his job. The rest of us began yelling the song with such gusto that they could hear us at the other end of the school.

With kindly Mr Johnston driven to assaulting the kids, we were clearly becoming a handful. Things at home were partly to blame.

7

THE LAST STRAW

Mum had worked through many of her personal challenges by this time. Her braces were off, she'd successfully completed her Masters in Psychology, and Joshy had grown beyond that awkward phase of needing constant supervision. Unusually for a mother of four, there was not a single sign of ageing upon her. In fact, she was often mistaken for Juliet's sister, which was quite eerie, like a female Dorian Gray. For all that, she was not happy.

New boundaries were being negotiated but the lines were still unclear. Dad was drinking more and losing his temper every few weeks, despite Mum threatening to leave him if the outbursts continued. Around this time I walked into Mum and Dad's room and caught the last of Mum's sentence: '… you promised. I made love to you last night.' I gathered from her stroppy tone that sex had become rare and was now being held out as an inducement or favour. The solace Mum had drawn from the love of the girls was evaporating too, because Juliet was spending more time away from the house. The excitement of Juliet's new friends was hard to compete with, and this must have been hard for Mum, who prided herself on her youthful magnetism.

Like Mum, Dad appeared from afar to have a blessed life. By some measures he was middle-aged at this point, as his back injury had shown so dramatically, yet he remained an early riser and a hard worker – a man who projected an air of vigour. His hair was still thick and red, his voice strong, and his beard made him look like a Viking.

Dad's professional life was at its zenith. The youngest member of a high-profile radiological partnership on Macquarie Street, he was making serious money. He and his partners had made headlines a few years earlier when their CT scanner, the first of its kind in Australia, had been winched through a hole in the practice wall, holding up traffic in the process. His views were even sought on the radio, and between the work of his booming practice and the consulting services he provided to Sydney Hospital, there was enough cash to pay off a 20-room house, and buy a Porsche and a big boat.

Dad was a proud man who'd always expected a certain level of respect from the world around him and his growing professional success meant the world was now delivering. He was a heavyweight scientist with a prodigious memory for facts and wide-ranging literary, historical and artistic tastes that meant he could lay claim to being a genuine polymath.

But the pressures in his life were intensifying. Feeling increasingly shut out by his wife, working stressful days in town and spending hours on a grinding commute all drove him to self-medicate in the evenings with alcohol. A man who was ill-suited to parenting found himself with a bunch of lively children and a perpetual hangover. His strategy for managing that situation was mainly shouting, which was yielding diminishing returns. Mum's enthusiasm for the role of peacemaker was wearing thin, too.

Sensing that the mood of the house was turning, Dad attempted to get more involved in parenting. He volunteered to take me and my sister to the movies on Sundays. When the first of those promised excursions rolled around, Dad rose a little hungover and began cooking eggs in the kitchen. I got changed over the heating vent, so excited I could barely tie my shoelaces. Dad looked back over his shoulder to see me fiddle with the laces. 'You still do bunny ears?' he chuckled indulgently. I felt embarrassed that I hadn't learnt the proper technique.

Soon Ren and I were ordered into the Porsche, and we were slopped around in the back of that uncomfortable thing as Dad drove it hard to town. (He admitted to me years later that the car was an expensive shitbox that handled as if it was missing a wheel.) I emerged green and shaky on the other side, but the promise of yum cha before the show was enough to quell my nausea.

Yum cha was still exotic in the 1980s. It could only be found in Chinatown, and The Nine Dragons was the restaurant of choice because there was always a chance of spotting a television personality on a good day. Today was just such a day. Within minutes of being seated, Dad spotted the actor Garry McDonald.

'You know Norman Gunston? He's famous,' Ren explained in awed tones. 'He's eating dim sims!'

But the thrills didn't stop there. Dad poured scalding Chinese tea with a shaky hand and trolleys brought us food unlike anything cooked at home. Among the stranger things circulating, I spotted chicken's feet. The sad wrinkled offerings looked like something from a biologist's specimen jar.

'Give you 40 cents if you eat one,' my sister dared me.

'All right,' I said, determined to appear brave, though the pre-vomit rush of saliva had already entered my mouth. Forty cents could buy two bags of mixed lollies at the milk bar. I steeled myself for the ordeal, but it wasn't so bad after all. The withered brown skin fell straight from the bone and tasted like Kentucky Fried Chicken, which was my only other reference point for fine dining.

Stomachs distended with dumplings, we set off for the movies on George Street. Dad picked a movie he wanted to see – *Murder by Decree*, which was about Jack the Ripper on a night out. It didn't strike us as strange that Dad was taking us to a horror movie about a weirdo eviscerating prostitutes and we dutifully sat through the whole thing. Dad left satisfied and drove us home with the righteous glow of the dedicated father, while we sat in silent trauma, knowing we would go sleepless for weeks.

Looking back now as a father, I can recognise these outings as a master stroke of parenting, and I've used them myself – soothing Chinese food for a hangover, a quiet air-conditioned environment, and no need to talk to the children. I know that our father loved us, but I don't think he really liked us, at least not in the sense that he wanted to talk to us when we were little. It was an ingenious scheme for avoiding any interaction with us on these new Sundays when he was the designated carer. Unfortunately the plan came unstuck on the very first outing.

Getting out of the car once we arrived home, I stupidly closed my door without checking which side my sister was exiting. For such a small car, the doors had the weight of a prison gate, and one of those great lumps of metal closed with a very final clunk upon my sister's thumb. Her finger was mashed into the metal grooves and she shrieked in agony.

Dad leapt straight into doctor mode. He concluded that the rapidly growing bubble of blood under her thumb nail needed to be released, and the only way to do that cleanly was to heat a large safety pin over the stove and jam it into her nail. We all stood in a ring in the kitchen, looking on aghast as he removed the glowing red pin from the hot plate and moved it slowly towards Ren's mangled finger. It would not have looked out of place in a James Bond torture scene. But the pin never got to her because she fainted, falling hard against the kitchen cabinets and banging her head on the way down. She'd scored a busted head to go with her crushed thumb. Dad performed the grisly puncture and iced her head while she groaned and dozed.

His medical duties discharged, Dad turned the last of his unspent adrenaline upon me. 'You never close a door on someone, you idiot!' he yelled. 'This day has been a trial from start to finish.' He went on to excoriate me for my selfishness, and even my embarrassing inability to tie shoelaces. We had gone from a morning where everything shone brightly, and he'd been affable and encouraging, to this tirade, and I felt deeply destabilised. A few years later, processing this and other similar episodes, I think it was his tendency for revisionism which troubled me more than his temper. Had he really been so unhappy and just concealed it all along? In any event, his opinion was vulnerable to reversal and no approval could be clung to with any certainty.

I ran in tears from the kitchen, down the stairs, out to the back garden, then under the house – through the plumber's entrance to the basement. Here the giant water tanks dripped and the spiders crept. Here I could sulk in solitude and try to forget that I'd nearly removed my sister's thumb. As I calmed my beating heart, the central heating system rumbled to life. It pushed out delicious columns of warm air through the vents in every room upstairs while I sat in cold darkness. I thought of all the times I'd perched on one of those vents, reading *Fantastic Mr Fox* until my bum was branded red with stripes.

I felt the sadness of things past. A box of matches sat by one of the clay pipes – a legacy of the days when Mark's smoking had been clandestine. I struck one now in his honour, but its lambent light shed no warmth.

A rush of strange aquatic noises burbled through the plumbing. Thinking of the sermons which I was hearing on a weekly basis at school, I imagined that I was in the belly of a whale, black as a coffin, with only the muted sounds of the ocean to soothe me. The god of the Old Testament could be scary. Now I imagined I had some insight into what it must have been like for the Israelites to have suffered in one of the Lord's spasmodic fits of retribution.

After a time in the gloom, even I got bored of self-pity, and I judged that peace had probably returned upstairs. By now Dad and Mum would be out of their minds with worry, I hoped, and sorry for ever having driven me away. I returned with an air of righteousness – they had wronged me but I was big enough to put an end to their torture. Mum was cooking dinner, Ren was doing her homework. Neither of them even looked up from what they were doing.

Dad's attitude was worse than indifference – he imposed an Arctic freeze between us, refusing eye contact for two whole days. On the third, he asked me to clean up the study, where Ren and I had watched a VHS tape the night before. I dutifully rearranged the pillows and picked up cups, but Josh plucked one of the pillows off a chair and began gently batting me with it from behind. Not even bothering to argue with him, I pushed Josh out the sliding glass door, closing and locking it behind him.

Now I was free to put the last touches of order upon the room, but Josh set up an incessant wail, banging on the door in outrage at his exclusion. Just as I bundled up the last of the mess and went to unlock the door, Dad appeared behind Josh, with a face like death. I fumbled at the lock with a trembling hand and Dad burst in upon me. I barely had time to draw the first breath of explanation before he'd boxed me on the ear. I was rocked to one side.

Like most children of the 1970s I'd had spankings before, usually for making too much noise in the stairwell or being disobedient. Sometimes the hits were delivered on the spot – me swinging from Dad's hand like a gymnast, trying to avoid the hits. Others came after banishment to the bedroom, with whole minutes to think about the belting before it came – sometimes delivered with an implement on the back of the legs or the arse. But a hit to the ear was new and I had no strategy for managing it. All I could do was cringe in a ball on the floor. I remember shouting 'I'm sorry sir,' as if I was at school. It was over as quickly as it had begun. And he was gone.

A hush fell upon the house that evening. I felt as if some foundational pillar had been removed from family life and I waited in silence for the edifice to fall. In my room after dinner, Mum asked me to explain the fight with Josh. No doubt Dad had seen enough of me tormenting the poor kid in the last few years to have lost all sympathy for my version of events.

That night I lay in bed, unable to sleep. With my head against the pillow, my pulse beat loud in my ears. It sounded like the ominous fall of footsteps on the stairs. My muscles were rigid as I ran the options for escape through my mind. I wanted reassurance, but I would have to traverse the house at night to get to my parents' room, and I wasn't even sure how they would receive me. I imagined I could almost hear them arguing, all the way up there.

In a last effort to retrieve our splintering family, Dad booked us a trip to New Zealand. We flew to the South Island and rented a campervan for driving through the mountains on our way to Milford Sound. I was sufficiently diverted by the scenery to forget about family dramas for a time.

One evening, Dad told Ren that she would be minding Josh tonight, so he and Mum could go out to dinner. He went into the small bathroom cubicle for a shower, but burst out again soon afterward, in an agitated state.

'My ring's gone. Have you seen my ring?' He spoke urgently but quietly, to avoid alerting Mum, who was up the front, retrieving our pyjamas.

'I'll find it!' Ren had the sharpest eyes in the family, honed by years of jigsaw puzzles, and she jumped at the opportunity to win Dad's favour. She found his wedding ring so quickly after taking to her knees in the bathroom, that Mum was still riffling through the luggage out of earshot.

'You clever girl!' Dad lifted Ren off the ground in ecstasy. 'You can have anything you like. What do you want? Something from the shops in town?'

'I don't know,' Ren giggled in amazement at her golden transformation.

'Well think about it and tell me later.'

When Mum and Dad returned from dinner, Ren whispered her heart's desire to Dad – a little charm bracelet that she spotted in a nearby store. He simply nodded and squeezed her hand.

The next morning we bought Ren's bracelet, scoured the shop for other trinkets and enjoyed a soup by the window with a spectacular view of the mountains. When Dad ushered us back into the van, his pre-drive nerves were humming. We sat in silence for the first 30 minutes of the day's drive, when Ren suddenly blanched and jumped up from her seat.

'Dad,' she said in a panicky voice. 'I've left my bracelet at the shop.'

'How did that happen?' asked Dad.

'I don't know,' my sister wailed.

'You stupid girl,' he said, without taking his eyes off the road.

Ren sat back down slowly, trying to process her stunning fall from grace.

Only years later did I appreciate the symbolism of the lost

ring, or the irony of the whole episode – a man who got angry at his daughter for losing a bit of jewellery that she'd won for finding a piece of jewellery that he'd lost.

8

NEW LOVE

After coming home from our trip, Juliet took Mum into town for a night out. In between sets from an awful band, Mum was introduced to one of Juliet's new friends, Caro. A few weeks later, Caro attended Josh's third birthday at our place and although there are photos to prove it, I have no memory of meeting her then. None of us was formally introduced to Caro that year, so her impact upon us was minimal. Her impact on Mum, however, was profound.

If you subscribe to the view that love only occurs when people are open to it, then my mother was a yawning barn door. Part of me resents the dishonesty of people staying in an unhappy relationship right up until the next love comes along. But in Mum's case, the inherent complication of children provided an excuse. She told me years later that her first nights out with Caro had an incredible ease to them, and that alone made Caro irresistible.

Within a few months my mother had already decided what

to do. She would leave my father, take the remaining three children and move in with Caro. But her communication of that plan left a bit to be desired. As is so often the case, the resentment over our broken family unit came us much from the way it was handled, as the break-up itself. Mum explained it to Dad as a separation, rather than a divorce, which I believe left him with the mistaken impression that a reconciliation was still possible.

As for the children, Mum moved us out without consultation or even explanation. She told me abruptly that she was leaving Dad, which was very upsetting, despite my fear of the man. In a matter of days, the house was packed and we were preparing to move into a new place, about a kilometre down the same road, with a new parent I'd never formally met. The whole episode was rendered even stranger by Mum's insistence on emotional transparency and the fact that she and Caro were both qualified child psychologists. I don't think Mum's approach can be found in the family separation handbook.

In the middle of the moving preparations, Mum drove Ren and I home from the shopping centre where we'd replaced those few household items that needed an upgrade. Ren sat up front, with me behind. The Volvo whistled while we stared out our passenger windows.

'So we won't be going on family holidays any more,' I mused sadly, revealing the full extent of my shallowness.

'They were stressful anyway,' Mum countered quickly.

She was right, of course, but I thought it was callous of her not to acknowledge my loss of idealised trips with a mythical happy family.

'Don't you have your French test on Monday?' Mum asked Ren, in a transparent attempt to divert us.

Ren was doing French that year, in deference to Mum's wishes, but her spirit of independence was finding expression in passive resistance.

'Let's speak French for the rest of the trip,' said Mum. Judging from Ren's posture, Mum may as well have just suggested we stuff broken glass up our bums. Beyond the motivation to bolster Ren's vocab, I imagine Mum was relying on the fact that Ren's lessons didn't cover parental separation.

'I don't want to, Mum,' said Ren, crossing her arms and glaring into the distance.

'En Français,' Mum answered calmly.

'I don't feel like it.'

'Je n'en ai pas envie,' Mum corrected her. It sounded much less sulky in French.

'Stop it,' said Ren, becoming angry.

'Arrête ça,' said Mum, almost smug now.

The atmosphere had shifted and I was becoming unnerved. Trapped with a mad linguist, Ren tried the only avenue available – escape from the car. We pulled up at set of lights and Ren made to leave. She was quick, but Mum was quicker. She held Ren's seat belt catch in place with her steely wrists. Mum rarely lost her temper, but when her wiry frame whipped to anger, she assumed the look of a witch. The lights changed and Mum drove again, one hand still on my sister's belt.

'Stop it,' said Ren tearfully, banging on the inside of her door. She was soon sobbing in defeat.

'En Français,' Mum repeated.

But Ren's high school French didn't extend to concepts of false imprisonment and human rights abuse, so we endured the rest of the ride home in the universal language of silence.

Back in our empty house, the tension was no better. Dad and Mum clearly had a number of administrative issues to resolve but neither had the stomach to do it, so Dad went under the house to clear the last of the tools and neglected sporting equipment. I had mentally farewelled all the rooms of the house, bar Dad's study. With him downstairs I took my chance to stand one last time in his private space. The carpet had indentations from the entertainment unit which had housed his television and video recorder. I thought of all the time he'd sat in this spot watching the ABC, interspersed with league finals (provided there was the prospect of Ray Price and the Parramatta Eels grinding out another shit, low-scoring victory in the mud).

Some boxes, full but unsealed, lay in rows by the door. At the top of one box was a familiar plump red photo album and I flicked through it. A shot from Cardinal Avenue, the house before this one, showed me on all fours in the garden, apparently posting a dandelion up the bottom of a cat. I didn't remember doing that. A shot of me in a car in Europe, my pudgy hand intercepting food intended for someone else. An echo of something rang here. It was overseas that my first images began. Perhaps for adults and children alike, the thrill of foreign sights and smells burns something more permanent on the brain. Dad's fellowship in Oxford meant we had travelled for a year when I was a toddler.

Over the page I began to feel tearful. There was a photo of Dad with his young medical colleagues, sprawled on picnic rugs in the muted English countryside, smoking pipes and wearing tweed jackets, caps and scarves, as if they were reenacting a scene from an Arthur Conan Doyle novel. They were undeniably glamorous. A few shots later my father almost looked bohemian, with long hair and a cord jacket, leaner than I'd ever known him, bearing me on his back as we walked the woods of France.

In the pictures of me, Ren and Mark, we were always clustered together and perky, like meerkats. I thought I could remember the slinky feeling of their parkas against mine, during that French winter, though surely these adventures were rehearsed recollections, repeated so many times in the Roberts oral tradition that I could no longer distinguish between my memory of us and the children I'm told we were. Even the images in my mind were coloured by a 1970s Polaroid stain. I imagined that light itself in the 1970s had a yellow tinge, and the hyper red of my sister's polo-neck or my brother's impossibly chocolate hair just reflected a world that glowed more brightly back then. The shots of us at this time, our obvious love and unity, together with my dawning awareness of the fractures that could never be healed now, brought on a kind of wrenching nostalgia – nostalgia for a time I never really knew. Chipped trinkets, like my sister's French skiing badge, and Chinese whispers from a trip long gone, were enough to make me cry.

Then I remembered those things that we had not repeated so often: being smacked for licking a cake that had passed by, so temptingly close, on a waiter's trolley in Paris, or being hit with a belt for sword fighting with Mark. This last one was vivid enough to trigger a blush. *The Three Musketeers* was the hit movie in Paris during that trip and we'd been given two perfect plastic rapiers, which we'd put to use duelling in the corridors of our hotel. I think it was my thoughtless indifference to fellow guests that triggered my father's temper more than anything else. Dragged to our rooms by Dad's fearful trembling hand, I remember the shaking alone rattled us into silence. I'd lain awake that night, my backside throbbing and those elusive swords calling to us from atop the cabinet where they'd been placed out of reach. I'd told no one of that memory. It had sharp edges. My tears dried and I knew it was time to leave.

The next morning, we loaded the last of our things into the car, drove across the railway bridge and down the valley to our new home. I'd only seen it once at an inspection where my mother had spoken quietly to the vendor, who had just lost her husband to cancer. The house looked dark, Edwardian and slightly forbidding. Caro was at the front door to greet us.

PART 2

MUM AND MUM

9

CARO

Caro had a short, practical haircut (though the light perm and rinse were too delicate to be butch) and a short, practical body to go with it – neat and compact, with powerful legs that looked as if they could deadlift. I decided her button features were pretty, and there was kindness in those eyes, though the prim set of her mouth suggested something of the martinet.

'Smart casual' was probably the kindest description of her outfit. She wore slightly baggy jeans with high-end sneakers and a white polo shirt. It was the look of someone middle class, conservative and sporty. Not really calculated to impress a young fan of the ska scene, but I imagine she was more focused on impressing my mother than me.

Caro greeted Mum with a hug and gave Joshy a familiar pat on the head. Then she shook hands with me and said hello in a pleasant contralto voice. It wasn't a traditionally feminine sound.

Less than a year earlier we'd bought an Alsatian called Annie. Mum had insisted on getting a female in the belief that they were more biddable and placid. Not long after growing out of her puppyish form, Annie had dispelled that myth by gnawing right through our guinea pig cage and devouring Mr Gladstone's replacement. From then on, we had been very nervous about Annie's interaction with the outside world and this was a particularly difficult test because Caro had her own dog at her feet – a worried looking kelpie.

The two creatures sprang upright, rigid and tense, before moving quickly into a tail-sniffing dance. They spun several rotations, nose to bum, then burned off the remaining agitation by chasing each other around the front yard. 'Caddy,' said Caro, with a warm laugh. 'She'll be fine.' The garden presented a number of obstacles for them to navigate – a fat kentia palm and a neat series of paths that wound tightly through flower beds in the Japanese style. It felt cramped and fussy after the sprawling expanse of our old place, and the dogs collided as if to confirm it.

Caro held open the front door for us and we all filed in, though Mum craned back for a last nervous glance at Annie, the role of peacemaker too ingrained to shake off. We were shown our rooms as if it had been preordained. There was none of the raucous 'bagsing' of rooms that normally accompanied a holiday 'takeover' by the Roberts clan. Mum and Caro got the largest room, with elegant French doors that opened onto a verandah. Ren was in the room opposite them. Cavernously high ceilings, pull-cord lights and leadlight windows created the impression of a stately Edwardian ball.

We had to traverse the house and climb a flight of stairs to reach the self-contained, apartment-style accommodation that would be home for me and Josh over the next ten years. This part of the house looked like an afterthought. It was cheap and flimsy, with iridescent orange carpet. None of the dark grandeur of the ground level had made it up here. But I think I was already grateful for the separation and appreciative of the light that flooded though my own verandah doors. So this was the new divide – girls down, boys up.

In the following weeks, Mum and Caro worked to make the place their own. Mum bought her own mini toolkit from the hardware store and bravely took on the job of patching elderly floorboards on the verandah. Caro stripped the wallpaper from the downstairs bathroom and began layering new material whose colour and shape I could only imagine, given the door was barred during the renovation.

The only man needed in this burst of construction was Antonio, a sweet Italian gardener whose services we'd occasionally used at the old house. This time, his brief was to build a new brush fence and he began this task by digging deep holes for setting the corner posts in concrete. The holes were done by mid-morning, when he turned his attention to the concreting, removing great heavy bags of the stuff from the back of his ute and schlepping them up the path. Not a young man any more, Antonio's legs seemed to bow outwards and his gait began to sway under the strain. He stopped in the blaze of the sun to strip off his flannelette shirt, revealing a white singlet and the most luxurious beard to ever grace a man's back. The hair climbed to the nape of his neck, where some bewildered barber had drawn an arbitrary line when cutting the sparser hair on his head.

'Phew, it's hot,' Antonio exclaimed, wiping the sweat from his neck with the shirt. We'd formed a sympathetic chorus on the verandah, and he smiled at us ruefully. Caro couldn't let this gentle man hurt himself. 'I'll help,' she said, and walked briskly to his truck. She returned just as briskly with a bag of cement over each shoulder. Her jaw was clenched but there was no other sign of strain.

'Phew!' Antonio exclaimed again. 'Sheesa strong!'

'She really is,' Mum agreed, looking on adoringly. She seemed to bask in the reflected glory of her lover's feat, wearing an expression of exquisite satisfaction that she reserved for those moments when the expectations of men were confounded. Antonio's expectations were not the only ones confounded. Our neighbours had expected a more traditional family to move in next door. Instead they got a pair of hot lezzos, one of whom could squat the weight of a small car.

The Andersons were our neighbours on the western side and they'd come around to introduce themselves the day before. Mrs Anderson had launched straight into her friendly 'welcome' spiel, while her husband had looked at each of us, clearly doing some arithmetic and concluding that Caro was not Mum's daughter. References to church and schools were politely bandied between our two very different tribes, and the Andersons had gone back out our gate, smiling but bemused. Mr Anderson may have been the most boring man in Beecroft (a hotly contested title in a field that included the late celebrity gardener Allan Seale). He also seemed quite dim, which was only remarkable because he operated on animals for a living and presumably needed to distinguish their back ends from the front. 'Don't let him operate on your dog!' was the only piece of advice my father had received from his friends at the golf club. For all that, the Andersons were incredibly kind and always made us feel welcome, even after they'd run out of alternative explanations for having two women at the head of a household.

If the Andersons had ever needed to use the downstairs toilet in our house, the true nature of our family arrangements would have been clearer from the start. A few days after the fence work, Caro unveiled the remodelled bathroom, saying 'This toilet is for girls'. The room was a collage, stretching from floor to ceiling, and it was comprised entirely of pictures of women, many of them nude. Joan of Arc brandished a sword alongside Annie Lennox's masked face. Annie, in turn, gazed intently upon Venus' naked form as it rose from a clam. Marie Curie and Gertrude Stein exchanged severe looks above the toilet, at which point I concluded that I probably would have suffered stage fright too acutely to use the toilet in any event.

Other people swore off more than just the downstairs bathroom, and abandoned our household altogether. We had a housekeeper, called Mrs Durham, who had helped us with cleaning once a fortnight at the old house. She'd lived through World War II and had the smoking habit to prove it. In addition to cleaning like a dervish, she was a dab hand at amateur vaudeville – on the occasional afternoon when she'd looked after us, Mrs Durham could always be coaxed into assaulting our piano, pulling out her false teeth and generally hamming it up with a phlegmy smoker's cackle. But now we'd moved into the new house, Mrs Durham only did one afternoon of cleaning before declaring to my mother that she couldn't, in all good conscience, continue working for a family that lived this way. It was the first sign of open hostility to Mum and Caro. Mum concealed it from us by explaining that Mrs Durham had retired.

By this time, Caro and I were locked into our respective positions – rivals for Mum's attention. We'd climbed into our trenches and neither of us could be dislodged without serious loss of face. Mum told me, years later, that Caro resented the privileged position I occupied in Mum's world. I suspect it was more complicated than that. Caro also resented my laziness and Mum's willingness to do everything around the house. We were also quite similar in our toxic mix of pride, stubbornness and emotional constipation. Caro was capable of warmth, something I could see right from the start in her interactions with Josh. But not with me.

I began to avoid the elegant space downstairs, keeping to the boys' enclave above. Josh and I bonded properly up there, and soon I began to think of myself as a surrogate father for him. I'm not sure how this deluded notion arose – anyone relying on me for role modelling was in serious trouble. And besides, Joshy had no need of additional parenting, given Mum and Caro were doing a fine job already.

Weirder still, on the few occasions when I did have cause to come downstairs for violin practice or dinner, I tried to give Caro such a wide berth that I was christened 'the human huntsman' for my habit of splatting against the corridor walls to avoid any physical contact. There was no hiding from the fact that I was having some difficulties adjusting to my new home. And to compound those difficulties, I was about to start high school.

10

EARLY HIGH SCHOOL

A day before classes began, my mother and I went up to the college for parent–teacher introductions. Mum's short-cropped hair and pencil-thin trousers wouldn't normally rate a mention and didn't register with me at all until I saw one of the teacher's reactions. Mr Steele, a frightening, stooped man responsible for discipline in the senior school, actually turned to stare in disapproval at my mother's appearance. Of course, this was catnip to Mum.

A number of key points were stressed in the interviews, especially the importance of adhering to the school's code of values (which, as far as I could tell, revolved around the celebration of sporting prowess) and Christian beliefs (except the inconvenient ones about poverty, humility and forgiveness). I got the feeling that we were hearing a more forceful version of the usual lecture because they saw Mum as a troublemaker. If only they'd known she was gay. They were also nervous about my older brother's example, given he'd been suspended several times just the year before, for devoting more time to his haircut than his reading.

But it was too late for the school to reconsider – I was already in. The next day I was shown to the Year 7 locker room along with 100 other new starters. The buildings for our year were older than the primary school and mostly underground. They could have been railway depots for all their grey air and sad metal. Our lockers lined the damp, subterranean corridors and hundreds of unbroken voices squeaked off the hard surfaces. I was given a terrifyingly adult timetable, which I was responsible for managing, and I was placed in 1P, the class for bright boys, well away from all the friends I'd made the year before.

My new classmates included Don, a hard, monosyllabic country boy of Latvian descent, and a plucky little scraper called Rick. Don and Rick quickly became my allies, and valuable ones too, as both were quick-witted and dominant.

By the end of the week we'd had a class with each of our new teachers, and I couldn't decide if our new world owed more to *Oliver Twist* or Lewis Carroll. Each teacher had devised their own peculiar method of crowd control. For the very camp Mr Martin, language lessons were managed by the threat of spelling lists. He could quickly turn from belting out a French song in his fruity tenor to issuing an enormous body of written work in punishment for a stray giggle.

'Have a one stroke two,' he would decree in his careless, prissy fashion, as he half-danced to the tune, meaning some poor boy had the choice of copying out two junior spelling lists or one enormous senior one by class time the next day. 'Make it a hot one,' he might add, meaning the punishment could move from one relieved lad to the next if there was another infringement during the lesson. It was a brilliant mix of fear and fun. Recognising the need for silliness in children, he indulged us with class recitations of the Latin verb 'to make' – allowing the conjugate form 'facit' (pronounced 'faark it' by all young Australians) to be shouted at full volume.

There was a similar homoerotic tinge to Mr Morrison's geography lessons but with none of the charm. Mr Morrison was the swimming teacher and insisted on wearing pastel shorts – 'tropicals' so tight they cleaved to his groin and provided perfect testicle separation. His understanding of geography stopped at directions to the page numbers of the textbook. I only remember one illustration on the blackboard and that was an outline of two sheep having sex. 'You know what goes in here, don't you boys?' he said, winking at us and pointing to the loins of his cartoon sheep. I wondered if this was really the education my father had intended for me. Mr Morrison shouted periodically and threw books out the window, probably resenting the knowledge in them.

Mr Harp preferred hard raps on the knuckles and seating boys on the 'invisible' chair by the wall, inevitably leading to physical collapse (which was sort of funny) but occasionally to emotional breakdown too (which was less funny). Silence stilled the room when a boy began shuddering from the exertion. Then came the tears, in huge dignity-shredding gulps, while all of us sat mute before this embarrassing torture, knowing the boy's fate could be ours at any time. Mr Harp kept his strange sadistic tendencies well hidden beneath a mild exterior. I remember his delicate aftershave and manicured hands.

Mr Milton ruled German lessons like a prison camp. Any word out of place and the offending child was hauled from the room by the ear. Any rocking on chairs and he would boot the chair, with full adult savagery, from underneath us. Entire lessons would pass with no noise other than the soft squeak of his leather shoes. Such a repressive environment forced children through the gaps that remained available for mischief, like a high-pressure hose.

One kid with an egg-shaped head began writing 'foetus', 'afterbirth' and other anatomical words on the blackboard before teachers entered the classroom. Don took to defacing my textbooks, turning every available face, including the pig on the front of my copy of *Animal Farm*, into a Rastafarian with dreadlocks and a spliff.

By the end of the year, puberty had taken hold of 1P and the nature of the graffiti changed. Rick drew dicks on the boys that featured in my French textbooks – pictures of smiling Parisian students, innocently seated around cafeteria tables, were transformed into orgy scenes. Giant cocks crossed over lunches to wedge in the mouths of talking teens. I remember the difficulty of resale time, when all my textbooks were inspected by a young lady to see if they were of a sufficiently high standard to pass to the following year's students. Her eyebrows rose sharply at the page showing a gendarme coming in great liquid paper fountains over the pedestrians. 'Got it like that,' I muttered, and examined the floorboards at my feet.

Sex at this point was still confined to the page, as we were getting precious little of it from the intriguing girls at the sister school, Loreto. Only my tough friend Nate had the courage to ask one of them to 'go round' with him, and he'd earned a kiss for his troubles. He chose the footbridge over Pennant Hills railway station for this romantic moment, which we all witnessed in awe and envy. The only other kisses I'd witnessed recently were between Mum and Caro.

11

PUBERTY

Mum's attitude to sex was embarrassingly open. She supplemented the sex education class I'd received at school by explaining the function of vaginal lubrication and other excruciating details, while I fought the urge to stick my head under a pillow. She also confessed to loving men and women equally, being more swayed by the attraction of the individual, regardless of gender. In the context of sex education, perhaps this was her way of saying, 'It's okay if you're a poof, Tobes. Sexuality takes many forms.' In retrospect, this was a stunningly enlightened position to take in 1984, given many schools are still struggling to adopt this approach even now.

Around the house, Mum was the more demonstrative parent. Beyond the affectionate cuddles and kisses that we all saw, Mum was happy to surprise me with more intimate moments. On one occasion when I made the mistake of coming into their room announced, Mum pointed to Caro, who stood awkwardly in her underpants. 'Look at those tits,'

Mum crowed triumphantly. Caro covered up quickly. She was generally more coy, which I put down to her being a Catholic virgin (something she'd happily confessed to us over dinner in our first few weeks together). Though, to be fair, it may have simply been that she didn't feel like showing her breasts to a creepy adolescent.

When Mum or Ren teased Caro about being a 'convent girl' with no experience of men, she noted for the record that she had received a marriage proposal from a nice young man when she'd worked as a supervisor for summer camps overseas. I got the sense that she turned him down gently by saying she wasn't ready, rather than confessing that she would never be ready for anyone with a penis.

At those same camps, Caro had refined her tennis game, progressing from a muck-around player to a seriously good amateur. When she invited me to a singles match on our neighbour's tennis court this became another forum for testing my assumptions about sex roles. I accepted, feeling as if there had always been some kind of unspoken challenge between us.

We warmed up with some ground strokes and it quickly became clear that I was in trouble. She planted her feet well, and swung her big racket through the shots with a powerful swivel of her shoulders. I was hard pressed to get the ball back over the net, let alone put anything on it. We were on different levels and the first game showed it. She served with slice and venom, drove me to the corners of the court, and left me panting in useless pursuit of shots that were so heavily laden with top spin they jumped up from the court and stung like a bee. Beaten to love in the first game, I could only hope that my serve would offer something in reply. It didn't.

When Caro pounced on the lollipops I threw her way, I had to adjust by serving as hard as my mighty 50-kilogram body would allow. I wound up and cracked each serve with an impressive whip-like sound, straight into the net. Knowing I couldn't compete from the back of the court, or the front, I figured I could concede quickly, under the guise of a 'bad serve day', and make some loud sounds with my racket along the way.

This strategy did have the virtue of ending my embarrassment before it could fester. Caro stood in confusion while I sent my serves all over creation. Her service games where just as fast – the ball was rarely impeded by my racket as it skipped neatly from my feet and onto the fence. Only one of her serves stopped dead on my side of the net, arrested in flight by my testicles. I'd misread the slice and wore the full brunt on my sack. Both too repressed to talk about it, Caro said 'Uhh, nasty!', while I skipped from one foot to the other and held my breath. It is tempting to think of this mishap as a symbolic representation of Caro's ball-busting nature but I should point out that our neighbour Mr Godfrey did exactly the same thing to me a few months later, and I don't imagine he was anything other than an enthusiastic supporter of nuts. It was simply my unique return of serve.

I walked home in ignominious defeat, trudging a few steps behind Caro. She turned to me and said kindly, 'You'll be dangerous when you get that first serve in.' Looking back now, some of my discomfort around Caro probably stemmed from my preconceptions about masculinity – something I've never been able to completely unpack. She could be quite aggressive when it came to sport, and even the fast, jerky way she drove her car suggested maleness to me. She was very strong and Mum often praised that quality in her. I think I felt emasculated by all this, especially at the age of thirteen when my father had faded into the background and I was left groping for guidance as to what it meant to be a man. Caro's homosexuality was more overtly political than Mum's, too, in that she would only watch women's sport, filled the house with books about the great women of history and generally conducted affairs in the house as if men did not exist. It also fed into an insecurity that was being stoked at school about my skinniness and violin playing.

I understand now that I unconsciously rebelled against the climate at home. By Year 8 I was sporting a blond 'flat-top', listening to edgy rock and roll, pretending to be tough, tightening my friendships with boys like Nate and embarking on a futile program of weights in an effort to make my manliness incontestable. Luckily, I had my sister's softening influence to help steer me through. Often impatient with others, Ren was always gentle with me. 'You're a good student Tobes. Most people would kill for

that. And you look like Mick Jagger. Don't worry about it.'
I wanted to hug her.

Ren played along cheerfully with the new family arrangement
but, like my brother Mark before her, she was just counting
down the days before she could finish school and escape from
home. I'm guessing she found interactions with Caro a bit
stilted, but you'd never have suspected it to see them together,
laughing and chatting so easily. Ren was the consummate
social performer, masterfully concealing any unease. Not that
she had any discomfort over Mum's homosexuality – she'd
accepted that as entirely normal years ago. It was more a case
of a strong woman wanting her own space. So this would be
the last year of my teens that I would share with her.

12

DAD'S NEW PLACE

Around this time, Ren said she was worried about Dad. She was the only one of us who'd given any thought to his state of mind, and for a moment I felt guilty about my self-absorption, before getting back to thinking about me. Ren told Mum and I that she'd taken Dad shopping for some essential household items, including a toaster. Dad stood paralysed in front of the shelves, so overwhelmed by all the turmoil in his life that he had no bandwidth left for trivial choices. 'Do you like the red one or the cream?' Ren asked him gently. He looked forlornly at the display and eventually said, 'I don't know. You decide.' It broke her heart to see the fierce father of our childhood meekly surrendering decisions, so broken by everything that had been taken from him.

After Dad was set up in his new apartment in town, Ren continued to check on him and she concluded that he was drinking too much and not eating properly. When Mum and others echoed this concern, Dad responded by eating and drinking some more. His body responded by stopping his heart. I'm told it happened down at the snow with no hospital for hours in any direction. He was choppered out of a mountain village in the middle of the night.

It was a minor heart attack in the end and Dad quickly settled back into bad habits, quietly confident it would all be okay. Mum, on the other hand, was quietly confident he was going to die, so she urged me to spend some more weekends with him, just as my little brother had been doing since the separation. Up until then, I think Dad believed things had been irreparably soured with the older kids, so he focused his efforts on getting it right with Josh. I'm sure he was nervous about seeing me again. I had some misgivings too, but I liked the feeling of superiority I got from affording him another chance.

When the first of those weekends rolled around, Dad instructed me to bring my violin. Perhaps sensing my deflated tone on the other end of the line, he added as an afterthought, 'Oh and you can bring a friend if you like.' So Josh, Rick and I set off by train on a Saturday, bound for edgy Kings Cross. Only 200 metres from the seedy swill of the station exit, the towers of Potts Point rose up from the end of Victoria Street like giant versions of the battleships that rocked gently at anchor behind them. Dad owned the penthouse suite at the top of Hordern Place, sharing his lift with barristers, real estate kings and importers of cocaine.

Rick made a whistling sound when Dad showed us in. The

place was all metal edges and glass, with minimalist furniture to match, but the view over the botanical gardens and harbour provided the soul to fill this spare frame. Josh wasn't awestruck in the slightest. He moved nonchalantly to the TV and asked for takeaway food, slotting straight into the sad rhythm he and Dad had established the preceding year. Under the glamour of this backdrop, Dad had been eating microwave dinners and growing steadily sicker.

A combination of our time apart and the feel of the place seemed to accentuate the usual reserve between us. The white marble floor reminded me of a modern exhibition space where you aren't supposed to touch anything. I paced the living room, looking at the pictures on the wall. There was a photo of my grandfather, Jack, in his later years, still handsome and square-headed, holding one of us in a swimming pool. I couldn't conjure anything of the man now, just a soft, kindly presence, though I remembered Dad saying he was a headmaster with an authoritarian streak that strayed into bullying.

Other photos of Dad showed him in front of various rural backdrops, travelling country New South Wales in the wake of Grandad's high school appointments, his red-haired complexion slowly freckling in the sun. Cleary the tallest of his brothers in these shots, and probably the brightest too, it was easy to see Dad as the golden child, but life with his father can't have been easy. There was even a photo of my great-grandfather, looking weirdly similar to me, especially around the slug-lips, and I remembered being told that he was a prick. Perhaps a scary father was a legacy we'd all had to shoulder, along with our chicken legs.

Not knowing how to initiate a conversation with Dad, I felt relieved when his colleagues knocked on the door. Dr Marsh, one of Dad's partners at the radiology practice, was a sweet older man who loved music, so Dad had suggested I play for him. I didn't recognise the other man.

I set up my music on a makeshift stand against Dad's empty fruit bowl and took out my violin. A simplified version of Mendelssohn's famous violin concerto was well under my fingers at this point and I was able to give the performance an extra lift with the acoustics of the bare apartment. Dad stood proud and formal to one side. I was satisfied with the effect but also vaguely humiliated, maybe because I thought I was cooler than the violin by then, or maybe it was just the indignity of being a performing seal. Those resentful feelings grew when it became clear that Dad's colleagues had no regard for anything I had to say.

'It's the right sound up here, isn't it?' I offered. Silence. 'For a Romantic piece, I mean.'

'Hmm yes,' said the unknown doctor. 'With a sunshade for that outdoor area, this could be the perfect place for Barry's 50th,' he said to my father.

A few more of my attempts were left to fall to the marble floor and I could feel myself shrinking. There was only one way to restore pride and exact revenge.

I found Rick in the second guest room, unpacking his Walkman. 'They're snobs,' I said. Rick nodded and pulled a patrician face to mock their expressions during 'musical appreciation' time. 'You seen the balconies?' he nodded to the one off our room. We walked out and leaned over the banisters to gaze at the road fifteen floors below us. We exchanged a smile and headed back out to the dining area where Dad had laid out a roast chicken and some salads that he'd bought from a store. Josh looked disappointed that it wasn't McDonald's.

Rick and I loaded our plates and took them back to our room. We threw our potatoes off the balcony, at first trying to hit the roof of the building across the road. When we went back for seconds and thirds, the gown-ups chuckled at our adolescent appetites. We tipped the next wave of salads over some innocent pedestrians as they trudged the footpath below. The thrill was too intense to give up. Now all the things in Dad's spartan fridge were fair game – including devon and a frozen bread roll.

Timing was hard to master, but eventually we could judge the trajectory of an object with the oncoming motion of the target. People were peppered, parked cars stained and verandahs across the road festooned with cherry tomatoes. Rick struck a couple in evening dress with a tub of yoghurt, which must have hurt from that height. We pulled back and crouched below the parapet, giggling like preschoolers. 'You think that's funny?' a man shouted in a rage from below, his voice swirling up like paper rubbish on the breeze. 'A little bit,' Rick answered him in a whisper.

A few minutes later there was a polite tap on the door and

two policemen explained to my father that there were reports of things being thrown from the upper floors of the building. They asked if he'd seen anything unusual. He hadn't, but we had. The unusual sight of vanilla yoghurt enveloping a tuxedo was hard to forget. The police politely took their leave and we decided to quit. Once the adrenaline had played out of our systems, we asked Dad if we could go to the store across the street for a can of soft drink. He was happy talking shop with his colleagues and handed me some coins.

Night-time in this part of town was very different. The criminal air of the streets almost made my skin tingle. We tried to buy a small pack of Benson & Hedges with Rick's weekend money but the man smiled and asked for ID. Out on the sidewalk an Aboriginal man played the didgeridoo for coins, and a homeless man lay nearby on a blanket. My fear fell away when we retreated inside Dad's shiny tower block. Back home in Beecroft on the Sunday afternoon, I told Mum that it was surprisingly fun at Dad's place.

13

OMA

The following weekend we had a visit from Oma – Mum's mum. Oma was an illegitimate child from a time when those things still carried a stigma. I think the devastating guilt complex she held onto had something to do with the supposed sins of her mother.

Oma loved us completely and when we were younger she'd performed child-minding duties in deadly earnest. The load of responsibility, together with the endless accident permutations that spooled across her naturally anxious mind, meant she was positively faint with exhaustion by the time Mum and Dad came home to relieve her. Occasionally the risks had been real – I remember her stalking the downstairs corridor, preparing to bludgeon a funnel-web to death with her sensible brown shoe.

For a time she had even lived with us, taking the granny flat under our old house. She'd slept in a small monastic bunk; by her bedside was a book borrowed from the library.

There was something quaint and humble about her habits. Interrupting her early bedtime preparation could produce a squeal of violated modesty if you caught her in petticoats.

At the time of her visit to our new home in 1984, Oma had moved into a group of units for older people nearby. It was not exactly a retirement village but only one step removed. I hadn't seen her for almost twelve months and she appeared to have collapsed slightly like a deflating ball. I gave her a kiss on the cheek in greeting and her skin felt loose. With my hand on her back, I could feel her raised vertebrae, like a dinosaur's skeleton. A little unsettled, I shifted up to pat her shoulders but they felt frail as well – I was worried I'd put a hand right through that paper-thin wall.

Oma pointed out the window at her cream Datsun and whispered, 'A young man drove up beside me and said, "Get off the road you old cunt."' She relayed this news in humourless horror. I wasn't sure Oma knew the meaning of the word.

'What were you doing, Mum?' asked my mother, while Caro laughed uncomfortably.

'I was driving down Copeland Road,' said Oma indignantly. 'Very rude!'

'I'll make you a cup of tea,' said Mum soothingly.

'Should I call somebody and report it?' Oma always needed Mum's guidance.

'No, just forget about it,' said Mum, putting on the kettle. 'How's Teddy?' she asked, knowing Oma's cat would cheer her up. Her life revolved around that indolent ginger, who stunk her place to high heaven.

'Mrs Crighton, next door, was standing on my lawn, looking in,' Oma was whispering again. The rules of her compound forbade animals, and she talked as if the management committee might overhear her. 'I'm keeping the curtains drawn now.' She had convinced herself that the neighbours knew her secret.

'And Mrs Thompson said to me, just last week "I'm speaking to management next month." Do you think she means to report me?'

'No, she's probably just speaking to them about the rubbish bins.'

Oma didn't look reassured. Every conversation with the neighbours had to be dissected for weeks to reveal hidden meaning and veiled threats. Purple conspiracies grew in Oma's airless unit, with Teddy silently imploring her to save him.

Watching on from the kitchen table, it seemed to me that Oma's mental state was more unusual than before, maybe accelerated by living alone; or maybe she had always been like this and it was simply clearer to me now that I was older.

Silence had settled on the room, and I think Oma could sense that she was being appraised. 'I'll do pick-ups,' she said, referring to the dog poo on the lawn, which she seemed to take some weird meditative pleasure in removing. Being active helped to arrest the worry.

'But your tea's almost ready,' said Mum.

'That's all right dear, I like it tepid.'

My mother shrugged and handed Oma some plastic bags. As soon as Oma had gone out to the back garden, Ren was impersonating the angry young driver. 'You old cunt,' she mock-shouted.

'Don't,' said Mum, laughing. She found it hard to see her mother recast as a figure of fun, because she'd known her to be tough and resourceful. Oma had raised Mum and Uncle Tony in a house with virtually no electricity or machines. All cooking, cleaning and heating had been a product of her ingenuity and hard physical labour. Mum and others in the surrounding houses of Galston (including a community of Germans who gave her the name Oma) had relied on her for a great many things.

Among other trials, Oma had survived a demented husband who piloted early biplanes, played the violin badly and enjoyed giving himself small electric shocks. He'd flown with the great Kingsford-Smith, despite being totally colourblind, and only avoided that last disastrous flight courtesy of a fractured arm from a riding accident (at least, that's how Mum paints it – Smithy was probably looking for any excuse to get rid of a mad co-pilot who couldn't tell the green bulbs from the red ones).

Even my father, not known for his charitable character assessments, conceded that Oma had been a wonderful conversationalist. All things I wished I'd experienced first-hand but never did.

'Can somebody help me close the back gate?' Oma called through the kitchen window.

'It's closed,' Mum sounded a little exasperated.

'No, no. The latch isn't down.'

'Will you, Tobes?' asked Mum.

I went to the back gate, where Oma wrestled with a jammed pin. She had bags full of dog shit by her side. Both dogs watched on curiously.

'The top latch is down,' I said, showing her. 'So it can't open.' I shook the gate.

But Oma didn't seem satisfied. One of those obsessional worries had her in its grasp. (To be fair to her, this particular paranoia was grounded in reality because we went on to lose two more dogs that way.)

'How about I put the dogs around the front?'

'Oh would you? Thank you Toby. I thank you. And the dogs thank you.' The relief on her face was like an opiate. The dogs didn't look thankful when I dragged them around the front, their paws drawing furrows of resistance in the dirt.

I went back inside while Oma continued fiddling awkwardly with the ground-level pin. Mum had laid out some biscuits to go with Oma's cold tea when we heard a muffled thud through the window. Caro was first out the back, the rest of us two steps behind.

Oma stood, looking startled, with dirt streaked down one side of her cardigan and face.

'Oh Oma. Are you all right?' Caro shouted in concern.

'What? I'm fine.'

'Did you fall?'

'No.'

'There's muck all over you.' Caro and Mum were both dusting her down now. 'Let's clean you up inside.' Caro bore her up gently.

I wasn't sure if it was pride or a head knock that prevented Oma from admitting the tumble. Back in the kitchen, Mum and Caro hovered over her protectively as she drank her tea and steadily revived.

As the evening blue crept down from the heavens, Ren came into the kitchen to say bye. She was headed to the movies with friends, and was catching the train to town.

'On your own?' Oma asked in shock. A new worry did more to revive her than the cup of tea. 'It's fine,' said Mum, trying to arrest the spiral before it began. 'She's with friends.'

Mum wanted Ren to grow up confident and unafraid. If she shared any of Oma's concerns about an attractive young woman walking home in the dark, she never let them contaminate her daughter.

Oma left not long afterwards, braving the drive before the light became too dim for her fading eyes. We were left to debrief over dinner, still chuckling but also wondering if we were starting to see something more serious. Mum relayed a chat she'd had with Oma's new doctor just the week before. Oma had answered 'no' when asked if she'd had any major surgery, only to reveal, in the subsequent physical examination, a mastectomy scar where her left breast should have been. 'Well, that's interesting. How would you account for the missing breast?' The doctor thought it was pretty funny. It seemed less funny now.

14

ViOLENCE

Troubled as she was by the changes in Oma, Mum was more troubled by the changes in me. By Year 8 the college had turned me into a little prick. Violence began at the top. My friend Don was addicted to smoking even before his family sent him to boarding school on the mail train from the country. He snuck out of the dorms for late night hits of nicotine, where the house masters periodically caught him. He was thrashed with good Christian zeal on so many occasions that he eventually wore multiple pairs of underpants at all times, to cushion the worst of the floggings.

The violence meted out to students flowed directly down the chain. Beyond the usual schoolyard scuffles, there were regular bag room 'pile-ins' where literally half of our year would squeeze into a dank 40 square metre room and jump on top of one another. I recall something partly comforting in that flesh cocoon, rolling myself into a defensive ball in keeping with the wisdom of avalanche survivors, hearing the muffled and panicky screams from boys shouting from the bottom of the pile, 'Get off. I can't breathe. I can't breathe.'

Most of us spent junior and middle school bruised from the shoulders down. We played the 'carton game', which involved knocking an empty Moove carton into the air until someone let it fall. That person would be hit as hard as possible by each participant. The stunning sequence of punches made a sound like a drum roll. More sinister was the 'poling' game. Anyone passing our lunch area who looked weak or had an objectionable haircut would be rammed groin first into a tree with their legs pulled apart. In retrospect, there was a primitive form of eugenics at work, a backyard sterilisation program for uncool boys.

There were so many acts of cruelty, which I would like to dismiss as necessary parts of jungle survival, but the truth is that some of those acts still cause me disquiet today. Crime number one – not content with throwing clay slurry from the art class at poor Stu Cumberland, I contributed to a gang tackle on that blameless boy. He looked like one of The Proclaimers and had a kind of brittle quality that clearly caught the eye of predators like us. Naturally he ended up crying after the assault. I then compounded the crime by talking my way out of the punishment while everyone else got caned to the point of tears. That was my style, split to the point of schizophrenia between wannabe tough guy with my peers and earnest good boy for the masters, most of whom spotted me for the faker I was and actually preferred kids like Don, who took it stoically on the arse.

Crime number two – teasing Michael McGuire about his high voice by helpfully pointing out at every turn that his balls hadn't dropped, just in case he hadn't noticed all by himself. Many years later I met him in a music store. Strapping, handsome and prepossessed, he recalled all the people who had given him such a hard time at school and I worried briefly that he might beat me and my earlier developing testicles to a pulp right there in the store. But he did something far worse, explaining with quiet dignity that his mother had died of cancer in his second year of high school and that it was the most traumatic time of his life.

Crime number three that year – spitting on gentle Mr Partridge who took us to the library for reading time. I devised a way to spit silently by laying a trail of saliva along the inside of my finger and then flicking it onto the target. It was celebrated as a breakthrough innovation by my peers and we perfected the art on Mr Partridge's old, bent form. He emerged from most library lessons with spit dripping from his tweed coat. I subsequently learnt that he too had been touched by cancer, losing two wives to the disease.

My friends and I were the most dangerous of animals at this point – fully developed faculties when it came to cunning and deception, but utterly unburdened by consciences, which were still stuck at the level of kindergarten kids.

At home, I was just as nasty. An endless barrage of negativity

and swearing came vomiting out of my mouth, especially
where my brother Josh was concerned. The one time I tried
to 'defend' him that year, it backfired. Our dog Annie was
obsessed with food and one afternoon she took advantage of
Josh's lowered ice cream to run her wet tongue along the full
length of it. Seeing Josh's look of horror, I kicked Annie in the
butt with my scuffed school shoe. Annie yelped and ran, Josh
cried, and my mother turned towards me in anger.

'You never hit the dog!' she said, grabbing my ear and
twisting it.

'Annie licked his ice cream,' I shrieked in pain. In my mind,
beating the dog had been a noble act. Shocked at Mum's anger,
and feeling unappreciated for my judicious use of violence, I
retreated upstairs to hide my tears.

Josh proved his capacity for empathy was more mature
than mine by coming up to check on me, and by convincing
me to apologise to Annie. We found her together and fed her
dog biscuits one by one. As well as a chance to make it right,
we were curious about the upper ceiling of her appetite (Josh
claimed to have fed her four cans of dog food just the week
before, which she'd eaten without pause). I could see Mum
through the kitchen window. She looked shaken as she talked
inaudibly through the issues with Caro. By the time they were
done, Annie had demolished a third of the jumbo bag and
took herself off to the back fence to throw it all up. Mum was
worried enough by my behaviour to book a double session
with my teachers at the end-of-year interviews.

The teachers agreed that I was out of sorts and asked Mum if everything was all right at home. I imagine she talked about the separation with my dad but probably not the sleeping arrangements with Caro. While everyone was in agreement that I was odd, they also agreed that I was surprisingly smart for a boy who'd had serious difficulty with spelling and sums only the year before. In fact, I'd topped my year. And while it's easy to be critical of the old Dickensian, cane-wielding reactionaries, not all of the teachers matched that description, and some even deserved credit for my academic flowering.

Mr Walton enlivened the famous engagements of the ancient world by sketching battle manoeuvres on the board, and got us to write first-person stories from the streets of Rome. Mr Black encouraged us to perform our own plays, collate anthologies of our stories and analyse lyrics from our favourite songs. These two men nurtured in me a love of history and literature that has carried me through life.

Mr 'Eight-ball' Jones, nicknamed for his prodigiously deep voice, had the knack of making science fun for children. He allowed Don to demonstrate the attractive powers of a statically charged ball by blowing cigarette smoke over it, wryly noting, 'You seem to have done this before, Don.' Rick was allowed to piss into a beaker for pH testing, returning proudly from the toilet with a frothing schooner of urine. And we all got to dissect rats' lungs, pigs' hearts, bulls' eyes and other nasties. You'd think the chopping and flaying would have been disturbing enough, but things deteriorated further after class when we began stuffing pigs' ventricles into each other's pencil cases and throwing offal at the kids on the lawn below.

Music with Mr Wallis (an ex-member of The Deltones) included a complete deconstruction of the songs on a Beatles album, and a chance to play some of those songs ourselves. I was also chosen to lead the school orchestra in all the musicals that year, despite being one of the younger musicians. I enjoyed the responsibility and the attention, and the music was well within my competence after all the years I'd spent with the Sydney Youth Orchestra. My mother thought I was the maestro and encouraged me to wear a purple velvet jacket to the opening night of the school's *Sound of Music* production. Everyone else was in plain black and I flush with shame even now when I think about it.

Other formative experiences from this time included our performance of *Noye's Fludde* (Noah's Flood). Halfway through that challenging musical, sections of wooden panelling began detaching from the ark on stage and falling into the orchestra pit. We battled on bravely through the giggles and thumps. The music master consoled us afterwards by saying that the school production of *Julius Caesar* had been worse – the dramatic death scenes were undone by a broken, flapping sword and laughing corpses.

All in all, I was learning important lessons about ensembles, as well as academic success. But good grades and public violin performances did nothing for my reputation, or the feeling of weakness that came from Caro's strapping example. I had to offset my nerdy image with some mischief, and luckily we were coming into party season as the weather grew warmer.

15

ALCOHOL

The first party that summer was a sad one to mark Ren's departure. She was relieved to have finished with her uptight Anglican school. With the HSC out of the way and her university course deferred, Ren moved to Newtown, in the inner west, with some true friends that she'd made outside of school in the last few years. Now in full possession of her statuesque physique, Ren had flourished into a charismatic beauty, and everyone wanted to be near her. It was time for her to see the world.

Mum would have happily kept her kids around her until she died, like one of those Italian nonnas with three generations living in a ring around the house. But she bravely accepted the need for each child to find their own way, and tried to hide her distress. She made a lumpy cake with unnaturally green icing and left it to cool on the kitchen table before going out to the back garden to share a glass of champagne with Ren.

'Congratulations on getting into science, Ren,' said Caro,

a bit formally. On the one hand, she must have liked the idea of fewer competitors for Mum's attention, but on the other, she may have been disappointed to lose the one child who actually pulled their weight around the house.

'Thank you,' said Ren. 'Maybe I'll specialise in the properties of gas. I feel like I got a head start with three brothers.'

While we talked, Annie slunk unobserved to the back door. She was cursed with a gnawing lust for food, would eviscerate bluetongue lizards on our lawn and eat birds (feathers and all) hard on the heels of an evening meal. She could open a fridge with her face, like a canine jewel thief, and even delicately remove a treat from its wrapping. The smell of baked goods was too much to bear.

We came back inside a little later to divide up the cake. Only some sad crumbs remained. At least a kilogram of food and several hours of preparation time had evaporated in a silent frenzy. It took us a few minutes to identify the culprit, who later added insult to injury by dropping a loose turd on the verandah that even Oma couldn't have cleaned up with a bag. Perhaps it was an act of protest at the ordinary confection.

The other parties that summer ended just as badly. My friends and I had discovered alcohol and we had a cascading series of options for getting it. Our friend Neil already shaved his face, so he was first choice for brazenly presenting at the Beecroft bottle shop. Neil occasionally passed for an eighteen-year-old, albeit one with an intellectual impairment. It only worked when the cashier had gone without sleep for a few days. On those golden nights when Neil left the shop and raised the bottles in triumph, you could hear our answering cheers from across the street.

The drinks of choice back then were 4-litre casks of Lindemans (which came with an inner bladder or 'goon' which could double as a pillow at the end of the night), West Coast Cooler (an alcoholic soft drink pitched firmly at our demographic) and Stones Ginger Wine (a sticky alcoholic mixer, not intended to be drunk on its own, for octogenarians who had grown tired of life), any one of which should have raised an immediate compliance flag when it was taken out of the fridge.

If Neil was rejected, say, because the cashier cared to look at him, we paid older boys to do it. Failing that, tough Nate could be relied upon to travel to the Star Hotel in Chinatown, where they would have happily sold liquor to primary school children. If Nate was grounded, someone would be chosen to syphon off whisky from their parents' liquor cabinet. After getting wise to that stunt, some parents had begun scratching a mark on the sides of their bottles; but more cunning still, we replaced the stolen nectar with water – something we could do once or twice before an angry father wrote a letter of protest to the distributor, decrying the quality of the scotch.

Most nights began at the Beecroft Village Green – part-playground with a few rusty swings, it also had some scrappy bush adjoining the railway tracks. We judged this to have the perfect charm and ambience for a night out. The first goal was to drink all the alcohol before parents or police could take it away.

Sculling rituals involved squeezing wine bladders into each other's mouths and 'shot-gunning' cans. Shot-gunning meant puncturing the side of a can, usually with a stick or knife, tilting the can upright with your mouth attached to the hole and opening the top. The air pressure works to push the fluid straight down your gullet. I remember the sweet, putrid rush of those sickly drinks squirting into my stomach, and the sour burpy injection of beer that would sit unsteadily in the gut for a few minutes, deciding whether to come back up.

On one occasion it decided to come back up in the most embarrassing fashion. We boarded a train bound for the city, and I took my seat with friends on one side and strangers on the other. The lurch of the train's departure triggered a mass evacuation from my stomach, where three 'shot-gunned' West Coast Coolers were at war with my mother's risotto. I clamped a hand hard over my mouth in a futile effort to arrest the stampede, but this only diverted the mixture to my nose. Dinner and drinks roared out of both nostrils, like the twin nozzles on a windscreen wiper, shooting across the divide and onto the feet of the commuters. Screams of horror filled the carriage. My humiliation was complete when peas blocked one nostril, leaving a solitary outlet for the remaining vomit, which burned across my nasal membranes on its way out – a single jet that narrowly missed the nice young girls who had jumped onto their seats to escape the flood.

There was a macho competitive element to 'shot-gunning', but a practical imperative too – alcohol tastes terrible to most teenagers and by using this method the mouth was largely bypassed. In dangerously quick time we'd be flying on the chemical and sugar rush, laughing in adolescent brays at the unexpected antics from friends who'd never revealed their vulnerability or stupidity so nakedly before.

Ironically it was big Neil who was often the first to lose coordination and speech, then nasty little Nicholai would challenge us to fights before collapsing in a bush muttering darkly, and Rick would bring us all back together by declaring his love for everyone. If we were lucky enough to have girls in attendance, Nate would usually snap and storm off after being rejected by one of them, and Don would take cynical pot shots from the side.

Over the coming months, Don lost his virginity in the bracken by the railway, Nate got caught stealing things, Nicholai punched out a stranger's teeth for no reason, we hid from police in sewer pipes, and parents were forever taking us home in disgrace. When the police did corner us after one petty act of vandalism (overturned bins), Nate rose gallantly from his hiding place to take the rap on his own, drawing attention away from the rest of us as we lay quietly behind a garden hedge.

The one proper party of the holidays was a shameful affair. One Saturday night, Don's new girlfriend Antonella went away with her parents and trustingly handed the house keys to her school friends. Of course, these girls invited a group of us back to the empty house on the understanding that we'd all be quiet and respectful.

The gathering quickly snowballed into a party, music went on, excitement built as boys and girls flirted. Outside in the garden, hip flasks of spirits were emptying too fast and a few tables were knocked over. Neil, who was normally tipsy but sedate, climbed onto the roof shouting, 'I'm a possum.'

'Yeah, sort of, I guess. You're breaking the tiles,' said Antonella's friends, sounding polite and nervous.

Earnest young Kyden, a cadet, deposited the first vomit of the night in the flower bed. Most of us would have been concerned at the wasted effort – love's labour's lost. But for him it was the loss of dignity that stung. 'I'm a jerk,' he kept repeating, echoing the refrain from the government's anti-drinking campaign as he retched.

Someone poured beer into the VCR, a chair was broken, arguments about the responsible treatment of Antonella's house were erupting around the party and two opposing ethical camps formed – the drunk and the sober. The neighbours made their first visit to investigate. 'Where's Antonella?' they asked. 'Not feeling well?' her friends tried it on. It was difficult to argue that a party atmosphere was appropriate for Antonella's convalescence. The police arrived, we ran, while others rode off on bicycles stolen from the garage.

We hid in the bushes. 'I can't go home tonight. We'll be caught,' I said, regretting everything. A helicopter passed overhead. 'It's the police!' In my current state of mind, that seemed like a logical use of law enforcement resources. Slinking home like rats, most of us survived the weekend without trouble. But on the Monday evening, I took a call from Antonella's mum, devastated at the destruction wrought by nice young private school boys.

I remember being interrogated and my voice taking on that strange, tight sound when I lied.

Had I been at the party? she asked.

Yes, it was lovely, thank you.

Did I know about the damage to their property?

I had heard something about that, and it was regrettable, though obviously I had no part in it.

Was I aware that alcohol had been consumed at the party?

Heavens, no.

Yes, there were fifteen hip flasks on the lawn, and one on the roof.

Many were grounded as a result, but not me. My liberal mother was only 'sad and disappointed', which actually hurt more than a thrashing.

In any event, party season was over, and it was several weeks before I saw Nate and Rick again – this time for a low-key session of records and cigarettes in the upstairs den of my house.

Nate had brought a litre of milk and gave it to Mum on the way in.

'See?!' she said, turning to me. 'That is so thoughtful.'

I didn't have the heart to tell her it was probably stolen. Upstairs, the three of us talked about the difference in mood between the old house and the new.

'Your mum is so nice, Tobes,' said Rick. 'This is the best house for hanging out.'

I was nodding along, happy to take credit for my mother's lax parenting, when Nate suddenly upset the universe.

'So your mum and Caro share a bedroom?' Nate asked, already knowing the answer. This was an explosive question. Years of hiding from this moment had been emotionally exhausting and suddenly I felt driven to get it off my chest. 'Yeah, Mum is gay.' I looked shyly at the 1980s carpet and envisaged things going a number of different ways, most of them bad. Nate and Rick leant in protectively. 'It's okay,' said Rick. 'My mum has a dildo.' It was a weird non-sequitur but I knew everything would be fine now.

'Your mum is beautiful,' Nate offered, sweetly. There was a long silence. 'I'd like to watch them,' he went on, less sweetly, looking wistfully out the window. 'Me too,' said Rick. The conversation was going to even stranger places than I'd predicted but at least I felt safe in the bosom of their friendship, and relieved that we were now examining their deviance and not my mother's.

Mum loved Nate and Rick as if they were her own, and

they were repaying her kindness with loyalty now. They'd given me licence to talk about Mum at last, so I told them of the girlfriends before Caro, Juliet helping to raise Josh, and the circle of women they'd seen at our house on various occasions. None of it seemed too weird for them to take. I wondered if Rick and Nate had already discussed it and were only seeking confirmation now.

The feeling of being unburdened was exhilarating. My peer group, and school generally, had such an ambivalent attitude to homosexuality that the result had been very hard to predict. On the one hand, 'poofs' and 'faggots' were shameful, detestable things. The words were applied not only to effeminate boys and cross-dressers like Boy George, but to anyone with a weak or gentle disposition. In fact, the term 'gay' was synonymous with bad or pathetic, as a number of friends had made clear when they said, for instance, 'Your room is gay'.

On the other hand, some boys at school pretended to kiss each other (with hands interposed between mouths), simulated gay orgies on the oval (albeit fully clothed) and called each other 'darling' so often that the mocking intent had been lost. A school so focused on sporting achievement and so denuded of the female sex (not only in the junior ranks of the students, but across the teaching staff as well) was bound to have homoerotic undertones. That said, not one boy at school had ever admitted homosexuality, as far as I knew, and doing so probably would have got them expelled. So I was right to be nervous about the way Rick and Nate received my news.

I suspect, in their minds, lesbians were such a different breed of homosexual they may as well have been straight. My mother was certainly a much less threatening version of homosexuality than the queens on Oxford Street or a gay rugby player, which would have been dangerously close to home. In many ways, she was the perfect entrée to this world of 'difference' in that she retained her femininity, had clearly liked men enough at some point to have had four children with one, and was genuinely loving in her interactions with me and my friends. It was not hard for them to accept her. And perhaps, less charitably, Nate and Rick were serious when they alluded to the old porno trope about 'girl on girl' action. I imagine it would have been much harder for them to be around two hairy dads, whose bedroom antics would have been the stuff of nightmares rather than sexual fantasy.

Once we'd all made that leap of acceptance, it wasn't long before we sought out more extreme examples of difference to test our middle-class limits.

Over the next few years I had more academic success, I was promoted to lead one of the larger orchestras in the Sydney Youth Orchestra, and I worked hard to offset the embarrassment of both achievements by behaving like a delinquent on the weekends.

Around this time my friends and I attended our first Mardi Gras in Sydney. The event had morphed from an edgy protest march that few people other than the gay community and Darlinghurst police knew anything about into a fun spectacle that drew a mainstream crowd. I'd like to say we went along to express our new-found solidarity for gay Australians, but I think we mainly went in the spirit of freak-show gawkers.

There were at least ten of us from school and our pack mentality lent the night a slightly feral air. A modest crowd lined Oxford Street to watch the floats and we stood on milk crates or hoisted ourselves onto the grilled bars of windows to get a better view. A procession of dancers and show-ponies strutted their stuff: hyper-muscular men in leathers, pretty boys in skimpy trunks and glitter, tongue-wagging glamour girls in tiny bikinis, butch dykes challenging the crowd to boo them with angry fist pumps. I'm sure it would look unremarkable and almost tired to contemporary eyes, but it still shocked and titillated in 1987.

Some of our school colleagues took verbal pot shots from the sidewalk and there was a sneering tinge to our section of the crowd generally, which I'm ashamed to say I did nothing to arrest at the time, though I remember feeling uneasy. The infamous 'grim reaper' AIDS campaign had been aired by this time and many heterosexual people felt that gay Australians were responsible for spreading this deadly disease among the wider population. Even educated people like my father were horrifically judgmental about the epidemic, which at this point showed no sign of slowing. Some of that fear and judgment was apparent in the jeers from drunken bystanders.

This was my first taste of flamboyantly gay Sydney, and I laughed along with Rick and the others. But it felt like something was missing. While I understood this was supposed to be a night for the gay community to let down their hair, it was quite an extreme and theatrical kind of homosexuality on show. I thought of my mum, who would have been mortified up on one of those floats – not because she was ashamed of being a lesbian, but more because she identified as a quiet, suburban mum, in a stable relationship. And I'm sure some of the people in the parade saw themselves the same way; my concern was more about the message received by people who had no other reference point for the gay community beyond the one on display that night. Those from more sheltered backgrounds needed to know that most gay people were boring Sydneysiders just like the rest of us.

That feeling intensified when I saw the coverage of the parade in the newspapers the next day. Salacious pictures lit up the front covers, including a tragic drag queen walking home along littered streets at dawn with one busted stiletto heel. Articles from Christian lobby groups protested the debasement of public morals, and it was clear that Mardi Gras did nothing to combat the misperception of gays as promiscuous and debauched. People like my mum were the private face of stable, gay life, and I wished the world could see it, if only to bring some balance to the debate.

That said, we were now hooked on the thrill of this new, glitzy world and the following weekend we snuck into the

Unicorn Hotel in Paddington, which played host to gay dance nights throughout the 1980s. Other than the odd bowling club, where the proprietors had lost their eyesight, there were very few pubs that allowed underage boys like us to enter unchallenged, especially given I looked like an underweight chihuahua. The Unicorn couldn't have cared less.

We walked through the front door, wincing in expectation of being bounced out straight away, but there were no bouncers and, as far as we could see, no restrictions on serving the inebriated either. The place was surging with drunk gay men. Soft Cell hammered through a set of woolly speakers, guys rubbed together on the dance floor or stood at the bar shouting to get over the music.

I can't say we were accepted as part of the gang. We were neither leered at nor salivated over. We were simply ignored. We were tourists, and they knew it. The only memorable interaction with the locals happened when Neil let the music and beer override his good judgment. He jumped onto one of the tables, took off his T-shirt and twirled it over his head like a lasso. I think the combination of his tensed torso and undulating pelvis was supposed to evoke a rodeo rider, but it looked more like someone trying to waft away a fart. A young man with a serious expression walked over to us and said, 'Please tell your friend to put his shirt back on.'

We caught the train back home that night, rehearsing a set of stories to wow the more sedate members of our class on Monday.

At home, the dynamic had shifted a little in the wake of Ren's departure. The natural banter that Ren used to fill the spaces was all gone and there was nowhere to hide from the awkwardness between Caro and me, other than the upstairs den where I was spending more time than ever. Maybe in an effort to bring us together, Mum encouraged me to accept a lift from Caro in the mornings, because her route into work went right by my school.

She drove her jumpy sports car with a practised hand, letting the engine rev to the point of protest before flipping the gears. It reminded me of those trips into town with Dad. And like those trips, these ones with Caro were also conducted in silence. But at least Caro and I could coexist at this point. Dad and I were virtually estranged by now.

On one of the rare visits to Dad's place that year, he took Josh and I to Darling Harbour, which had just opened its doors to the public. We walked aimlessly between the sterile white buildings, gradually growing weaker in the sun until Dad finally gave in to Josh's campaign for an ice cream. They entered the food court while I sat against its shady wall and breathed the cooler air.

When I'd revived and stood up, I saw that Dad had gone. No sign of Josh either. A little burst of adrenaline got me moving more quickly as I imagined Dad already stewing. I walked the entire precinct with increasingly frantic steps, and was on the cusp of calling Mum from a public phone when I spotted Dad's red hair on the pedestrian overpass. I took the stairs to the pathway, two at a time, and bounded up behind Josh. I gave him a tickle and placed a hand on Dad's shoulder in a vain attempt to jolly things along.

'Found you!' I said in false bonhomie. I tried to deliver it with enough gusto to put Dad off the stride of any rebuke. He looked at my smiling face and then stared straight ahead. I filled the yawning gap with babble about all the things I'd discovered on my walk. Several minutes into my spiel, he stopped walking and interrupted me. 'I think the best thing you can do,' he said, gripping Josh's hand tightly, 'is take yourself home on the train.' His voice wavered with the effort to contain his anger and he passed me $2 for the fare. 'Oh, okay,' I said, still trying to maintain my bright facade, though it was now more inappropriate than ever. He turned on his heels and walked Josh back the way they'd come.

The signal was unmistakable: we were to part ways at this point. I stood in confusion, heart beating fast. It was not always obvious what was required in these circumstances. Sometimes it was best to ask for forgiveness, other times it was better to follow instructions literally and simply leave. I took the last option, but it didn't work out well.

Dad drove Josh home that night and met Mum at the front door for the handover, where he spent a cathartic ten minutes telling her about the kind of boy she'd raised – one who cheerfully ran away from his father on city excursions, showed no contrition for any problems he caused, and looked like becoming a criminal. For someone who hadn't been spending much time with me, his assessment was remarkably accurate. Mum did all the apologising for me, making up for the cue I'd missed earlier. It was months before I saw Dad again.

16

GiRLS

Despite having such a close relationship with my mum and sister (and growing up with women all around me), I was particularly uncertain with girls. But 1987 was a big year because, among other things, I had my first proper relationship – that is, of course, if you don't count Alexandra, the most precocious reader in primary. Alex had confirmed that she and I were 'going around' together in Year 4. I was unsure of my duties, so I adopted the literal interpretation and followed her around. I was also confused about how to treat her – she was clearly a competitor when it came to reading and showing off, but engaging her on that level seemed to result in fewer kisses.

I stayed over at Alex's place one night and embarrassed myself, I think by wearing my Errol Flynn velvet boots. That spelled the end of our affair, though Alex was bored by then anyway. She broke it to me bluntly in the playground and I cried for a full lunch time, as much from my soggy tuna sandwich as the humiliation of being dumped. My mum noted years later that my reaction to the relationship breakdown was unusual for a child, choosing to read that response as evidence of exquisite sensitivity.

By early high school I had worked through my grief over the loss of that three-week relationship and was ready to love again. I'd studied Nate's technique: do something dangerous to impress the girl and then try to kiss her while her mouth was still open in shock. I didn't trust myself to jump from a moving train like Nate, so I played to my natural strengths – writing letters and drawing pictures. Occasionally this produced a polite written reply, but more often just some helpful verbal guidance on where I might improve my grammar or shading technique. The nice-guy persona that I cultivated, along with my art portfolio, earned me some pitying looks from the girls of Normanhurst, and absolutely no action.

It was going to take a very forward girl to break my high school drought – one undaunted by my timidity and chicken legs. Patricia was the girl for the job. One of the more sexually generous lasses on the North Shore, she led me (and later, some of my friends) on that age-old journey. When I met her at the Beecroft Village Green in 1987 she was sixteen, with cherubic cheeks and a cutesy voice, but there was already something naughty and knowing in those lazy, heavy-lidded eyes which belied the initial impression of innocence.

The weekend before, Neil had gallantly revealed to the group that he had 'fingered' Patricia, so she arrived that night on the loose understanding that she was Neil's date. Just how loose soon became apparent when she began kissing Rick, me and others, before settling on me as the temporary winner. She tasted like bubblegum and cigarettes and smelt like hairspray – a sweet plasticky scent from a can. Every now and then I smell something similar on a person in the street and it transports me with jarring immediacy.

I never asked Neil how he felt about me taking his date and at the time I don't think it even struck me as disloyal, although it certainly does now. Things would eventually come full circle, and I would learn that the start of a relationship sometimes offers some clues as to its likely end. But none of that was on my mind as Patricia led me off to a quiet section of the park for some serious tongue pashing. The others shrugged and resumed drinking.

All of Patricia's clothing was elastic, including a teen bra that was designed to help young girls when they were learning how to put one on, but also helped young boys when they were learning how to take one off. This was perfect for my nervous hands, as I explored with no boundaries in sight. I was wildly excited to be given a green light and she was very pretty. My good fortune was obvious to everyone in the park, including me. At sixteen I was more knobbly than ever – tortured with braces and a scrawny frame. My defining features were knees, nose, elbows and Adam's apple. I looked like a bag of triangles, so Patricia must have been long-sighted or even drunker than me.

I put my hand down the front of her leggings and she wriggled and panted while I inexpertly worked away. The eventual reward was a deeper journey into the bushes where she produced a condom. With its awkward slippery surface and my confusion over which way it unravelled, the condom may as well have been a Rubik's Cube. By the time I'd mangled it into position, any magic associated with the moment had evaporated. Not that there was much magic to begin with – just two pissed schoolkids rooting in the scrub like feral pigs.

I needed help to get things underway but she guided me patiently. I recall thinking that thrusting speed was a key performance indicator, poor Patricia no doubt feeling like a spectator to an individual sporting event. On the upside, the combination of whisky and a condom delayed climax for a surprising length of time, and cemented an impression of stamina in her mind which subsequent underperformance did nothing to erase.

When I'd finished (and I say 'I' because I'm sure she had not) we picked twigs and burrs from our backs, pulled up our pants and rejoined the drinkers in the park. Patricia was slightly bashful, while I was twisted by a curious mix of pride and shame. My friends received me with resentment, scepticism or congratulations, depending on whether they'd been kissing Patricia earlier in the night.

Don took me aside for a special debriefing session. Being from the country, where children take up that kind of activity a bit earlier in an effort to stave off boredom, Don was one of the few of my friends in a position to give me pointers for next time (e.g. 'You can take off the condom now'). He gave me a pat on the back and we took celebratory swigs from a bottle while Patricia stood awkwardly off to one side with a friend.

For all the excitement of the moment, less than 24 hours later I was crying on my verandah, stale alcohol working its way through my system, a feeling of foreboding growing for the week ahead, and a shattering sense of sacrilege for what I'd done the night before. The act itself had more of a mystical potency than I'd expected and I couldn't escape the conclusion that I'd cheapened it terribly, like mixing stolen single-malt whisky with warm Pepsi (which we'd also done that night).

I know these experiences are different for everyone, but in my case I found sex with strangers to be somehow damaging, at least at first. I'm sure with practice it becomes uncomplicated and fun. But I've never reached that point, and all one-off encounters left a stain that took months to process. In Patricia's case, I overcame my sense of disquiet and cobbled together an awkward relationship with her that lasted about nine months.

Guidance on how to behave around girls was sadly lacking at this point, and the attitudes of my friends towards girls were as ambivalent as their attitudes towards homosexuality. Anyone who had a girlfriend was usually so embarrassingly grateful to be in that position, they behaved like perfect gentlemen when the girls were around. But without a girl in the room to inspire decency, our conversations were appallingly sexist, stocked full of crude, shallow references we'd acquired from older boys.

For instance, after a barbecue where we'd met some of Patricia's friends from school, Don asked Nate if he thought they were a nice bunch:

'Did you like Louisa?'

'Nah, she's a pig.'

'Well, you don't look at the mantelpiece when you're stoking the fire.'

The best cure for this nonsense was genuine friendships with girls – something which gradually humanised us over the next twelve months, especially when we joined them as classmates in Year 11 at the college.

But for the moment, I was clueless about relating to Patricia. She was bright and mischievous, and while she set out to find the best in people she could also be wickedly judgmental. I wanted to impress her so badly, I tried to perfect a swagger for her benefit (which made me look like someone who'd just had a hip operation) and tried to smoke without coughing or grimacing. One afternoon she lampooned both affectations with such a deadly impersonation I had to laugh, even while I shrivelled up inside.

Rather than simply tell her how much I liked her, I showed her how fast I could run, how loud I could shout and how easily I could do her maths homework. Strangely enough, these demonstrations didn't work any aphrodisiacal magic.

The only performance which did have the desired effect was playing the violin at the Christmas Eve party at home that year. As an enthusiastic member of her school band, Patricia could appreciate musical ability and promptly dragged me upstairs to try to get some different sounds out of me. If I'd known the violin could be so useful I would have practised harder.

Halfway into this new duet, Mum's old partner Juliet came upstairs to say hi. I think she was intrigued by the thought of me with a girlfriend and probably wondered if I knew how to treat one, so she laughed in embarrassment to find me demonstrating that so badly. Patricia and I pulled the sheet up to our necks and watched Juliet retreat the way she'd come.

After a brief period of worrying that Mum would have to report our antics to Patricia's parents, it became clear that neither she, nor anyone else who came through our house, could care less that Patricia and I were having sex. In fact, Mum was genuinely happy for us and gave us plenty of space for the afternoon trysts that probably would have horrified Patricia's parents (had they known).

Physical intimacy was one thing, but talking was quite another, and our silences became quite desperate when there was no third party to moderate them. The presence of Rick and Patricia's friends helped to divert attention away from my social inadequacy. However, it became increasingly obvious on group holidays and outings that Rick was in love with Patricia. At first it was just horseplay in the surf, with Patricia insensitively informing me that Rick was very strong.

Later, Rick began a clandestine campaign of love letters and tortured songs on the guitar. To my surprise, Patricia showed me these letters without embarrassment. I think I was more bemused than hurt. I don't remember feeling any need to compete with Rick, probably naively thinking Patricia's choice was made, though that sounds more grounded and secure than I ever felt with her.

Eventually Nate did some detective work that uncovered something more between Rick and Patricia, and I tearfully confronted her for an explanation. 'Well, no one has ever written poetry for me before,' she said. I hate to think what would have happened if he'd written a novel. The betrayal took on an Arthurian grandeur in my teenage mind, with Patricia the Guinevere to my cuckolded Arthur. We reconciled briefly then split again when I learnt that Rick wasn't the only Lancelot. In fact, it was more like Guinevere with the whole Round Table (which would have made for a very different legend).

I played the aggrieved partner to full effect. In all honesty I couldn't claim the moral high ground, having fallen in love (albeit platonically) with one of her friends a few months earlier. In any event, I quickly learnt the power of turning away a suitor, sadistically enjoying Patricia's pleas for another chance and feeling my first sense of control in the whole painful business. Patricia would for a number of years afterwards regard me as some kind of missed opportunity –

a notion that would never have survived the banality of my company had she stuck around. As for my attitude looking back, I felt nothing but gratitude for a lively, fun girl who helped me along the road to being a better partner.

17

MANLiNESS

Thankfully I was in Year 11 by the time Patricia and I broke up, so I found distraction in the form of 100 teenage girls newly arrived at the gates of the college. After an indecently short period of mourning for Patricia, I was busily flirting with as many of them as possible. This scatter-gun approach didn't work, and once the more popular boys and girls had happily paired off I had to settle for making a number of new female friendships – something I should have tried much earlier. I learned to my surprise, that girls were happy to talk about much the same things as boys, and I gradually shed my social awkwardness, but sadly not the excruciating need to impress.

It was clear to me that larger boys were getting more attention, and unfortunately I still looked like a librarian. Insecurity about my shape was a complex issue. Beyond the need to impress girls, I was searching for some way to assert my manliness at home, both in response to Caro's example, and in an effort to prove to my father that I was no longer afraid of him. My neuroses were not helped by my peers who shouted 'Robo is a weed' whenever I walked across the quadrangle. I redoubled my weights program and drank raw egg and banana milkshakes twice a day. This strategy gave me gas and also yielded two small lumps around the biceps, which looked like I'd just reacted badly to a hepatitis injection.

I realised that I would have to do something else to prove my manliness, so I decided to take up rugby. Up to this point, sport had not been a rich hunting ground for me. I had played soccer for Beecroft up until about the age of eight, when orchestras began to fill my weekends. I still had vague memories of 22 small boys surrounding the ball in a congested mass, with dreamier kids like me staring up at the clouds while parents shouted shrill instructions from the sideline.

Athletics had been a better fit. I won a lot of races from ages twelve to seventeen and was one of the fastest boys at school, which surprised many people because I looked like someone staging a hunger strike and no one could understand how anything so pale and skeletal could walk to the toilet without expiring, let alone win a race.

The only other activity that was compatible with orchestra rehearsals was non-competition tennis. The school chose a quiet day of the week to drive me and the other dags to a tennis court so deep in the Ku-ring-gai bushland that no one would ever see us butcher the sport. Nate took advantage of the remote setting to hit his ball over the fence and then smoke cigarettes in the bushes while pretending to retrieve it.

Years of playing like this had given me the tennis 'basics' but not enough to prevent Caro from wiping me all over the neighbour's tennis court. Our semi-regular games were still embarrassingly lopsided contests. I figured that playing rugby would show Caro, Dad and others that I was a man, would allow me to use my pace, would win me the adoration of the girls in my year and would finally silence those taunts about 'Robo's violinist's physique'.

I signed up for the rugby trials that autumn and they put me through the usual drills along with everyone else. It quickly became evident to the selectors that I couldn't catch or pass and had no understanding of the rules, so I was duly placed in the 'fifth fifteen'. This team was comprised of the finest minds in the school. There were Latin scholars, debating champions, prize-winning art students and drama stars. Unfortunately, none of us could play football. Had we been required to interpret Shakespeare for the opposition there would have been no contest, but that wasn't much use when it came to 'taking it up the middle'.

In my first training session I was asked by the coach what I played.

'The violin,' I said.

'No, I mean whereabouts on the field.'

After that, Coach Gray made the decisions for me. He was a scientist and a hopeless footballer too, but he knew enough to put people like me on the wing where I would never see the ball. Our glorious leader was Bob, a very funny comedian who went on to write and star in a number of TV shows. He had legs that bowed the wrong way and a complete disrespect for the college's sporting cult.

One of the first drills for our backline involved moving the ball through the hands, followed by a 'chip and chase' for the winger. The ball was meant to go from Julian the chess champion to Bob the clown, then on to William the asthmatic for a kick that I was to regather and place in the corner. We tripped, fumbled, collided and kicked the ball to people playing on different ovals, until Coach Gray finally signalled for us to give up.

We jogged back breathlessly to hear his assessment. Bob asking eagerly, 'How'd you like that coach? Did it give you a stiffy?'

'Well no, Bob,' Coach Gray replied in his steady way. 'It didn't quite do that for me.' I still smile thinking about that exchange, though the memory has been complicated by Coach Gray's suicide a year later, for reasons we never learnt.

One of the many disadvantages about playing in the school's worst team was that we had to play first. This meant turning up around dawn on transparent wintry Saturdays. My rugby shorts ballooned out like a parachute over my musician's thighs. The skin on my legs went as pale as the frost on the pitch, except around my knees, where purple, discoloured patches throbbed in the wind.

My first rugby game was against The King's School. The other side had filed out to shake our hands and every one of them seemed to stand a foot taller than me. My resolution to stay out of harm's way was quickly broken when I had to catch the kick-off. The joy of taking that ball on the full was quickly moderated when four large boys jammed my head into the turf.

Afterwards, William (a kind country boy) began explaining that I could actually kick the ball away to avoid that kind of relationship with forwards in the future. But he soon realised from the drool around my mouthguard that he had better start with basics like my name and whereabouts. When I'd recovered a bit, I remember the most startling thing being the expressions on their faces: the opposition actually meant to do me harm, which came as quite a shock to someone who had only thought to do this for fun.

There was an air of panic that was primitive. Bodies slapped together and made an unexpected sound, like raw steak being dropped on the floor. My senses were heightened: the taste of dried spit, plastic and dirt; scared BO smells and eucalyptus liniment.

Trying to get into the spirit of things, I targeted one of the boys responsible for hurting me earlier and leapt up for a 'ball and all' tackle when he ran the blindside. I ended up clinging to his front like a koala and he continued running freely, ball in one hand, me in the other, while my teammates shouted, 'Around the legs Toby!'

I tried the legs thing a bit later and somehow mistimed it, copping the other player's studs in my face. I remember jumping up angrily and challenging the boy to a fight. Bemused at why someone had attacked his boots with their face, he just wandered off, having probably decided wisely that there was no honour in punching the crap out someone who was a foot shorter and malnourished. It was a day of difficult lessons.

The 'mighty fives' would go onto many more defeats, the worst ones at the hands of St Joseph's where we would play their tenths or twelfths and still leave on stretchers. Enormous numbers of Joeys students turned out to support these mismatched clashes by chanting arcane songs from the sidelines. More than anything I hated tackling their greasy bodies. Bad food in their boarding halls had unleashed a plague of acne on that strange school – God's wrath for hurting the innocent intellectuals of the fifth fifteen.

The best part about playing rugby that season was serving under our brave captain. Bob led us through a unique sequence of warm-up drills, right alongside the opposing team as they prepared in deadly earnest. 'Now hump the grass,' he shouted, with his pelvis undulating up and down. Our opposition stole some bemused glances at us and frowned as they tried to work out the advantage of that move.

We only won two games as far as I can recall, but one was against Knox Grammar when every other college side had lost to them. Bob made the only clean break of the season and couldn't resist a goose step to celebrate before getting to the try-line. This led to him tripping over and being smashed by the fullback. He was helped from the field but shouted words of encouragement as he left – 'Fifth fifteen, I must leave you now, but carry on without me. Attitude adjustment.'

My vision of impressing people didn't really work out. Occasionally some female friends came along to watch me bounce off the tackle bags at training, or see me stand idly on the wing until some larger boy squashed me into the mud. As for Mum and Caro, they were so distressed at the prospect of me breaking my slender neck or my violin-playing fingers that they didn't watch at all.

Football training and weekend games made it very difficult to maintain SYO, which actually suited me, because the violin no longer gelled with the macho image I was trying to cultivate, and orchestral pieces were becoming very difficult (especially for people like me, who no longer practised). At sixteen I'd been promoted to the largest orchestra, comprised of young musicians in their early- to mid-twenties who were all planning serious musical careers.

I was placed in the second violins, close to the front. Second violins typically get the grunt work of orchestral pieces, often tuneless rhythmic stuff requiring strong concentration and counting skills, neither of which were my forte. I was used to playing pieces without practice. Now I was playing devilish modern works with no conventional tunes to guide the ear of the lazy and gifted.

I shared my desk with a sweet older girl who humoured

me and didn't bitch about my lack of preparation. But one afternoon we were badly exposed. Fumbling my way through something I'd never seen, I noticed the conductor frowning at the rank sounds coming from somewhere in the orchestra. He went through section by section – winds, then lower strings, until he correctly identified the second violins as the source of the offensive noise.

I'd been fluffing the strings with breathy touches, looking with fake intensity at the music, hoping the conductor would admonish our section and move on. No such luck. 'Hmm. Something's not right in there,' he said as he motioned with his baton to the middle area where I sat. 'Let's go through desk by desk.' My shirt stuck wet to my back as the moment of truth descended.

When our turn came, I tried playing mostly with my bow one millimetre above the strings, leaving my partner to carry the passage as if the sound of one violin instead of two would not be noticed. But I couldn't even mime the timing convincingly. 'You better do some work,' the conductor said pointedly. The next Saturday we were demoted to the back desk, and I quit the SYO soon afterwards.

I still played in other ensembles because music was paying cash by the time I was sixteen. A few hours of work in a string quartet earned me decent money. I played at architects' functions, birthdays and medical conferences up and down the North Shore. I tried to impress Catherine, our cellist, by drinking beer at every opportunity on those nights. She expressed her mutual attraction by drinking water and going home as soon as we'd stopped playing.

The growing need to drink and be cool soon sounded the death knell for my music career, at least temporarily (later, it was the need to drink and show off that revived it). My formal violin progress stalled at a 'B' for my eighth grade exam and I never played regularly again. It upset my parents terribly, especially my mum, which gave me some kind of perverse satisfaction, although I can't fully explain why. I think I felt as if I was finally forging my own identity. Perhaps I was rejecting her overinvolved parenting or her embarrassing artiness. It's also possible that I wanted to distance myself from her as a lesbian at this point, because I now had a whole new crop of female friends who would have to learn about her and Caro. I couldn't be sure that my new friends would accept Mum with the same ease that Rick and Nate had.

But the motivation behind my move away from formal music wasn't all petty and shallow. I was smart enough to know where this life would lead and I didn't like what I saw. My teacher was one of the Sydney Symphony Orchestra's lead violinists and he hated his job. Morale in most Australian orchestras was appalling, players tended to be nerds, and there was absolutely no balance to their existence. These people played music at work, practised music at home and went to music concerts for fun. It's not a decision I regret when I see my former peers in the professional ranks. If anything, I feel vindicated by the number of them leaving music to become doctors and teachers.

But I still hear an echo of those early playing years whenever I attend a big performance night. I feel a hushed tingling wonder when the bells mark 'doors closing', and I see a ghost outline of myself around those players who queue in the wings, wearing their evening dress.

18

A TROUBLED BROTHER

The explosion of social activity that accompanied the arrival of girls to the school in Year 11, together with my need to be tough, meant studying took a back seat. I was able to maintain altitude for about six months, courtesy of all the academic fuel burnt in the preceding years, but I was in decline by the end of the year. When the academic results were tallied, I came in around fifteenth, which was a humiliating come-down from being dux the year before. I consoled myself that summer by going out with friends and drinking more.

The only interruption to that summer's intemperance was a holiday with Dad. His invitation to join him at the beach signalled an end to the big freeze that had grown between us since the Darling Harbour debacle. I was troubled by the idea of spending my valuable drinking time in the company of a man who didn't seem to like me very much, but on the upside, I was looking forward to seeing my older siblings, who'd also been invited.

Dad rented a place near Avalon beach with an arresting view of the ocean and enough rooms to lodge all of us. When I rolled up, Dad introduced me to his girlfriend, Amelia, an imperious blonde who drifted from lounge room to patio with a wine glass in her hand and a glance that seemed to hover about two feet above my head.

Ren was already there with her older boyfriend, Con, the manager of a pub in town where she was working. I felt a rush of comfort from seeing her face and we hugged for the first time in many months. She explained that she and Con had to go back to the pub for the Sunday shift, so they could only stay one night but would try to rejoin us later. 'Oh, all right then,' Dad answered in the brusque tones which he normally used to conceal hurt feelings. 'Here are some pamphlets for restaurants that will deliver. Have a look. Con, would you like a beer?'

Dad led the group to the sun lounges on the back patio. I stood awkwardly on the grass and listened as Amelia made stilted conversation with a rugby league-playing publican.

'So, you own a hotel do you?' asked Amelia, in her high society voice.

'Nah, I just run it. Good spot but.'

'Oh, is it near the central business district?'

'Glebe, near Harold Park, you know … where they race the dogs … and the trots.'

Amelia didn't look as if she raced dogs. It was becoming clear that their two worlds were separated, and even clearer that Amelia was uptight.

I later learnt that she was something of a 'gangster gal' who had dated some of Sydney's most colourful racing identities, so maybe she knew more about the dogs than she let on. This leant her some mystique after the holiday but at the time I just thought she was a nob. Dad was doing his best to mediate between the various players but he looked tense. I think he'd booked the house in expectation of genuinely reconnecting with his children, though it was sadly apparent that we were well apart.

When Marko knocked on the door, I looked up in relief. But he greeted everyone with eyes that were a little too bright and a voice that was a little too loud. Dad's embarrassment at his eldest son's condition seemed to ratchet up the tension even further.

'I've been recording with Jimmy Barnes,' said Marko. 'His voice is so loud it actually cuts out most of the spillover from the session musicians. We didn't have to put him in a booth.' He carried on with an elaborate explanation of the valves on the microphones and the properties of the human voice, without any regard for the mood of the room.

I was more absorbed in Mark's outfit than anything he was saying. He was now sporting a mullet, with a dyed portion at the back that ran almost to his bottom, like the tail of a giant racoon. Coupled with stonewashed jeans and loud red shirt, it seemed calculated to induce epilepsy. Typically, I took my cues from Marko as to where fashion was headed, but this time I was nervous about following. Mark was a sound engineer at Paradise Studios and was working on mainstream pop hits for the likes of Noiseworks and The Church, as well as cool underground acts like The Lime Spiders. My friends and I had scored signed albums from some of these artists and even smuggled ourselves into a number of their shows, which confirmed two things: rock and roll was the only sensible career choice; and my brother was a god. But God didn't look in great shape at the moment.

Dad didn't offer Mark a drink. Instead, he announced that everyone should get to bed soon and suggested that Mark might like to play a round of golf with me and Josh the next day. At the time I wondered if this was Dad's ploy for getting some peace, having decided that three hours of family time was quite enough. In retrospect I'm pretty sure Dad was just concerned about Mark's studio pallor and pink eyes.

The next day I phoned Rick early and asked him to meet us at Avalon golf course. Mark drove me and Josh to the course, stopping at the bottle shop on the way. Nine holes later he'd swallowed a fistful of Mersyndol and a bottle of Malibu, and began spraying balls all over the wrong fairways.

I've since looked up the product information accompanying Mersyndol, which says 'Paracetamol and codeine work together to stop pain messages from getting through to the brain'. I can tell you this combination stops some other messages getting through to the brain as well. The leaflet goes on to say the product includes 'Doxylamine, which is an antihistamine with calmative effects'. If unconsciousness is a kind of calmative state, then this is a good description. Though to be fair, the manufacturer probably didn't test the product with alcohol. Malibu is not on the list of things to avoid taking with the medicine, but it should be.

Confused and angry as to why his golf wasn't improving, Mark took to shouting at the scrubs which held his balls. Finally snapping after a unique sand-wedge shot actually pitched a ball back over his head, he threw the club away in disgust. Rick and I watched aghast as it skimmed over the green and cracked Josh full in the face. Like most eight-year-olds, Josh had spent the last hour bored and fidgeting, so a club in the face was unexpected. His screams brought Mark out of his chemical self-absorption long enough to conclude that I'd belted Josh with the golf club.

'You're always picking on him!' Mark shouted and ran over to attack me. The family perception of me as a bully was well entrenched at this point, though Josh and I got on quite well by this time. Poor Rick had to restrain Mark from bashing me. The feeling of being held firmly must have been soothing because Mark fell asleep on the spot and we had to drag him back across a mercifully empty golf course to get back to the car. We pushed him into the back seat like a corpse, and buckled Josh in beside him. I drove the car back to the beach house with no licence and only two driving lessons to my name.

Josh was white with worry as Rick and I walked Mark to the front door of the beach house, holding him up on both sides like a giant puppet. He shrugged us off angrily, slurred something and then tumbled over the stone threshold, striking his face on the hard floor with a wet slapping sound. We rolled him over in panic, quite sure he was dead. Josh cried as we carried Mark to a couch by a window, where Dad examined him. He lay in state for 20 hours.

The next day, Marko woke subdued, bruised, and sober for the first time in weeks. There was no family conversation about the incident, just more directions from Dad aimed at limiting our movements. I asked if I could go out with friends to attend a beach party, making it clear that I thought it very unfair we were all being punished for Mark's indiscretions. Halfway into my spiel, Dad made a throat clearing 'ahem' noise, which was always a warning.

'We're all getting early nights this week,' Dad said.

'But this is my holiday, you know, and it's not much fun … in the house.'

'Well, if you feel like that,' he said, 'you're better off going home.'

The Darling Harbour experience had taught me that I was supposed to apologise at this point, but I saw a childish opportunity to pick a fight, took the invitation at face value and left.

A few days after returning to the seclusion of my upstairs pad in Beecroft, Dad phoned to say that he was considering removing me from the college and placing me in the local public school because my attitude was worsening. I issued a thin apology for my behaviour and an unconvincing assurance that I would be a good boy from now on.

At the time, I felt as if he was willing to sacrifice my education before the altar of his pride. Now I believe he was simply looking for any leverage to keep me and Marko from becoming full-blown alcoholics.

19

CARS

In those days, there was nothing like a fight with my father to make me appreciate life with my mother. While Mum's 'hands off' parenting came with its own problems, the sense of freedom was extraordinary. As for Caro, she imposed some discipline (which I resented as fussiness) and also taught me the value of compassion at a time when I badly needed the instruction. Oma was a case in point. My grandmother's neuroses had ballooned as her mind deteriorated, and she was becoming such a nuisance that even Mum was running out of patience. But Caro always treated Oma with kindness.

Oma's reliance on the judgment of Mum and Caro grew as her own judgment declined. She called at least once a day to spill anxieties like a Catholic at confession. Her health problems were the main subject of those calls, though they were mostly a pretext for hearing a sympathetic female voice. She often relayed the details of her constipation and then rang again to itemise each symptom of the blockage, having forgotten the first call, and listeners would be taken through every element of a story that hadn't rewarded them the first time around. Mum started leaving the phone off the hook in the evenings.

Now and again I was caught by mistake in one of these conversation loops. 'Oh Tony, what are you doing there? It's wonderful to talk to you,' Oma would say, confusing me for her son, my uncle Tony. 'Yes, nice to speak to you too.' I stopped even trying to untangle the confusion after a while. 'I'm having problems,' Oma would go on in a more conspiratorial tone. 'Problems making faeces...' We all loved her choice of words, which made it sound like something you might do in a craft lesson.

If the phone calls didn't satisfy her, Oma could still visit us in person, driving over in her 1970s cream Datsun. That summer she came over for lunch and treated us to a master class in worry. She outlined the likely death of our dogs by road accident, and the almost certain death of my sister by inner city predators, until Mum decided we all needed some fresh air and moved us out to the back garden, where Oma hovered by the pool fence to ensure Joshy didn't drown.

Josh wasn't doing Oma or Caddy, Caro's dog, any favours. He'd worked out Caddy could be duped into a rescue attempt if he pretended to drown. By thrashing in distress and sinking to the bottom, Josh could work Caddy, and now his grandmother, into a state of apoplexy. Caddy swam out and circled above him, her little kelpie legs churning like a wind-up toy. When he rose to the surface, she scratched him and swam back to the stairs. Oma probably wanted to do the same.

'Do you think God wants you to be worried all the time?' I asked her, in the hope that an appeal to her piety might succeed where our many appeals to her reason had failed.

'God sends us warnings,' she said, considering my question without taking her gaze from the pool. 'And we have to listen to them.'

Well, I'd listened to enough warnings for one afternoon and decided to do something reckless instead. While Oma settled deeper into conversation with Mum and Caro, I went back into the house and grabbed Oma's car keys from the kitchen table. I figured I had ten minutes at least before me or the car would be missed, so I ran out to the street and stared at her Datsun.

It was not a pretty car. It probably hadn't been much to look at back in 1970, and the passage of time hadn't helped. An array of bumps and scratches, mostly at the front and back, spoke of Oma's new 'touch parking' technique, which involved parking without the aid of sight or sound. The sensation of impact was her guide. How she and other road users survived her driving was a mystery. My heart was beating worse than race day, but I felt certain that if she could make it to Beecroft, then I could make it around the block.

I jumped into the car and started it before I had time to change my mind. The noisy, uneven sound from the engine, and the hard plastic steering wheel with its quaint ridges, made me feel as though I was in a time capsule. The few driving lessons I'd had to this point were clouded by panic, and I juggled the gears and clutch clumsily.

A wild ride ensued (wild, at least, by my internal standards). Any bystander would have seen a worried face craning over the dashboard of an old car travelling at 30 kilometres an hour for the full 90 seconds it took to drive around the block. In nearly all respects my driving was indistinguishable from my grandmother's, though that was not my intention. I felt like a daring outlaw. The keys were returned and the crime was never discovered. I was hooked, like Toad from *Wind in the Willows*, and hassled Mum that very night to pay for a batch of lessons.

Some people say boys are either good at maths or good with cars. Well, I was good at maths. My approach to driving was a little bipolar – I continued to drive like a grandma most of the time, but also engaged in the most reckless idiocy whenever friends were involved.

It took me two attempts to get my licence. On the first attempt, I lost a record 44 points and was only preserved from further humiliation because the examiner ran out of boxes to cross on the form. My friends consoled me at school the next day by pointing out that another student had actually struck a pedestrian on his test. I guess there was no section on the form for that, either. But I secured my licence on the second attempt and Mum foolishly allowed me the use of her Ford station wagon, which I mistreated so egregiously it had to be sold twelve months later.

Random breath testing was only introduced in New South Wales in the 1980s and when I began driving there was still a macho drinking culture that almost dared young men to flout the law. The moral imperative to drive sober took a few more years to penetrate dense male skulls. Typical weekends involved drinking with friends and driving back from a party, drifting casually between lanes. Further elements of difficulty were sometimes added when friends climbed onto the car roof to do some 'urban surfing'. I shudder now to think how easily a tipsy seventeen-year-old driver could have clipped a gutter and sent everyone on the roof to death or permanent disability.

Rick and the others enjoyed hurling eggs while hanging halfway out the passenger windows. I would be blinking my tired eyes, trying manfully to keep the car in its lane while projectiles whistled out of every opening in Mum's car. Neighbouring cars would screech to a halt with egg-smeared Duco, innocent bystanders would yelp and scream 'Cunt!' as I drove by, and my passengers hooted and cheered.

I was eventually caught drink driving, then miraculously let off. After a long night at the Orchard Hotel, I performed a perfect U-turn across the Pacific Highway, up over the median strip (making an awful grinding sound) and on to the other side where a police car stood in full view to all but the dangerously drunk. The officer asked me to breathe into the white mouthpiece which I did everything to avoid, but finally blew enough pathetic puffs to give a reading of 0.2. He showed it to me, saying, 'Look at that.'

'Is that bad?' I played the ingénue.

He gave me a ticket for the U-turn and told me to leave the car by the roadside.

Most of my friends were not so lucky. Virtually all of them had one accident, sometimes more. Two friends were knocked out when their car split its bonnet against a telegraph pole. Another friend lost his ear on a highway, doing a neat roll. Luck eventually ran out for me too, and at Easter time in Year 12 I was involved in my first serious crash.

George Weaver, my friend from the early college years, took me to a party in St Ives. George had hardened into a tough footballer who liked a social drink, and that night he tested the upper limits of 'social'. By midnight he'd offended the party's host enough times to be challenged to a fight in the weights room. He walked out the front of the house and collapsed under a bush when it all got too emotional. You'd think having a driver who'd just been asleep under a tree would be the first warning sign. And having a driver who wore a T-shirt soaked in bourbon vomit might be the second. But it wasn't until George began taking the backstreet corners of St Ives at 110 kilometres an hour that I asked if he was okay.

Johnny Diesel's 'Crying Shame' was playing on the stereo, and the ultramodern digital speedo in the Mazda read 117 as George mounted the curb, overcorrected, mounted the other curb and slammed head-on into a tree. I remember feeling resigned and curiously calm as we careered towards those last obstacles. The first thing I did after the car came to rest was jump out and laugh in disbelief.

George didn't share the joke, partly because the impact had caused his collarbone to pop out. A group of men ran from a nearby party and challenged George to another fight, this time because of his reckless driving. I guess they figured that a traumatised kid with a busted collarbone needed a punch in the head to top it off. We could have stayed at the first party to get our beating and saved ourselves the car crash. All the way home in the cab the next morning, I was queasy with fear, and I've been a nervous passenger ever since.

With this crash, even my immature frontal lobe was starting to receive a dim signal from the heavens, and I began exercising more caution behind the wheel. But it took the most horrific crash to really ram the message home. At the tail end of autumn that year, my friend Nate (who'd left school to take up a trade) hosted a barbecue. When the sun went down and the party dispersed, a small group of us drove to Asquith Leagues Club to carry on with the night.

I'd only had two beers all day and figured they'd flushed through my system by the time I drove. Nate had quite a few more and none of us intervened to stop him from driving. Rick and I got to the club first and sat for hours in the garishly lit bingo hall, wondering why it was taking Nate so long to join us. I went to bed that night with a gnawing sensation in my stomach. The next day we learnt that Nate had crashed his car on the way to the club. He'd strayed onto the wrong side of the road and clipped the front of a car travelling in the opposite direction bearing a young married couple. The combined speed of the vehicles was over 100 kilometres an hour, and everyone was shattered on impact.

The young woman in the other car was pregnant. She died at the scene and her husband was hospitalised. Nate's legs were broken backwards by the car engine when it was shunted into the cabin. His legs were in casts for twelve months and he spent the next eighteen months after that in prison for the manslaughter of that poor woman. While there had always been a certain restlessness and frustration radiating from Nate, the accident permanently saddened him in some quiet, profound way.

Nate's parents, who were decent people, had to endure death threats from people who had been whipped into a frenzy of indignation by articles in women's magazines deploring Nate's murderous actions. I felt, and still feel, guilt at having suggested we go on to another venue that night and I live in fear of some karmic retribution to my loved ones. I can't begin to imagine the emotional work needed to climb back from the loss of your wife and child in those circumstances. My guilt was compounded by a twisted kind of pride that came from telling the North Shore princesses at school about my good friend who was in jail for manslaughter. This story gelled nicely with the lawless image I was trying to convey.

On a less shameful note, I stopped driving pissed. My only crimes after that related to the appalling state of my car. Figuring that a flimsy vehicle would do less harm to innocent road users, my father let me use one of the smaller leased vehicles from his practice. It was a box-like Honda Civic with pretensions of futuristic design that came off looking more like a bad prop from a *Dr Who* episode. Within twelve months the carpet had rotted into compost, the door edges had rusted through and the driver's window was permanently stuck a fraction from closed.

On the upside, this hapless conveyance gave me the freedom to take off and visit my new female friends whenever things were too strained or dull at home. Around this time, I was taking off a lot because Caro and I were drifting from an uneasy détente to a more warlike footing. Mum was deeply saddened by Nate's accident but Caro was more outraged at our irresponsibility. She was also becoming increasingly bolshie about my lack of effort around the house.

20

FRACTURES AT HOME

One Sunday in term two, I woke late to find a basket of my wet clothes at the top of the stairs. Caro was trying, in her subtle way, to disabuse me of the notion that dirty clothes are washed and dried by a magical fairy. But that was never going to work. I'd actually seen the magical fairy do the washing. Her name was Mum.

I took the washing basket back down the stairs to the laundry, where I'd seen the fairy do her good work before, and returned to my room knowing that a gauntlet had been thrown down, along with my dirty clothes. To avoid having to address the issue, which I could almost feel exploding downstairs beneath me, I closed my bedroom door.

An unusual tussle ensued, where Caro and I used the movement of washing as a proxy for human speech. I heard heavy footsteps climb the stairs, a thud of something being dropped, followed by steps receding down the stairs. I opened my door to find the washing had moved a foot beyond the landing – closer to my bedroom door. I moved the washing back down, but not wanting to inflame the situation irretrievably, I conceded the territory between the laundry and the bottom of the stairs.

By a series of moves, with neither of us ever seeing the other, we moved the washing up and back. Each move of Caro's brought the basket closer to my door, and each move of mine retreated further up the stairs. I had a new insight into the anxieties of the German High Command during World War I as they'd slowly withdrawn from the Western Front. My bedroom door was the Hindenburg line. If that was breached, it was all over. Thankfully, Caro wasn't as ruthless as Monash and retired, content, once I'd deposited the washing at the top of the stairs, right back where it had all started, before the needless suffering.

As I waited nervously for hostilities to resume, I heard an argument start up below. Even at this distance I could hear Caro clearly, though Mum's softer voice was a little harder to make out.

'He needs to grow up,' said Caro.

'I've told you before, I would rather do it. I have always done it for the children,' I think Mum said. She'd always believed that childhood was for dreaming.

'So we're running a hotel now?' said Caro. 'You're wearing yourself down.'

Something inaudible but pleading in tone, then – 'I find arguing with you more stressful!'

That must have shocked Caro, perhaps because it suggested that a life without her might have been easier for Mum at this point, despite all the work Caro did to lessen the burden around the house. More conciliatory murmurs, then something from Mum about my trial HSC exams. This was a knockout blow, because academic focus trumped everything for a pair of women who had worked in schools and celebrated learning above all else. It was clear to me that I wouldn't have to do any housework provided I continued to study hard in the lead-up to the exams.

The offensive was over, thanks to the intervention of some heavy artillery, and we'd settled a new accord. I honoured my end of that agreement by putting in a frantic burst of work before the trials and I did very well – back into the top handful of students who appeared on track to gain entrance to any university course of their choosing. But the effort almost broke something inside. I was feeling burnt out and utterly unmotivated. In some ways, a stellar result for the trials was the worst outcome because it convinced me that I needn't do much else between then and the HSC.

The fallout from the struggle at home wasn't immediately obvious. Mum and Caro appeared to be tighter now that they'd agreed new boundaries. But I couldn't shake the feeling that something had frayed between them. I felt no joy at the idea of them fighting, but neither did I feel responsible enough to do anything to fix it (say, by doing some washing). Caro and I were more awkward than ever before. So as soon as the trials were over I took off in my decaying Honda – seeing bands at the Sydney Cove Tavern, going on camping trips in the Royal National Park and staying up all night in the houses of my friends.

Social gatherings were by far the most exciting thing in my life. Our group of female friends were all beautiful and preternaturally poised by comparison to us boys, and with make-up could pass for fully grown women. The air at our parties had a sparkling quality and even a special smell – partly a function of my youthful nose, blooms from North Shore gardens, and the scent of the girls themselves, which still plays the faintest note for me now and makes me feel a tinge of melancholy for that lost time.

The drinking at these events was more restrained than the early years in the Beecroft Village Green, but it was marginal. While most of us could legally drink by now, our ability to manage the stuff was still in its infancy. The exaggeration of emotional states was more than many of us could bear and we justified those outbursts in a pretty unconvincing way.

Someone might kiss a friend's partner, and there would be the obligatory outrage, a court-martial comprised of mutual friends and some public shaming. Sometimes a genuine tussle erupted over intruders at parties, followed by endless recounts of the fight and congratulatory backslapping. Or tears flowed during an exchange about our 'difficult' childhoods. We blundered through our parts like amateur actors, looking to each other for emotional modelling. Should I feel this now? Is it okay to express it like that? While all emotional exploration in our teen years looked as awkward as the shoes on our oversized feet, alcohol seemed to expose the performative aspect more comically.

On the positive side of the ledger, alcohol also impaired the judgment of one of my female friends to the point where she kissed me. Suzie was an effervescent blonde who played the piano and loved literature. We were firmly part of the same social set and knew each other well enough to be relaxed when we chatted, which was half the battle for me. Almost as soon as we separated from our clinch, Suzie said she was certain we'd be together from the moment our eyes had met in music class the year before. I have since noticed a curious revisionist tendency in some women, that compels them to look for the hand of destiny in matters of the heart. The less romantic reality was that there were several equally lovely candidates with whom I'd formed strong bonds in those last years of school, the only thing separating them being a willingness to kiss me.

That being said, Suzie was a good fit. She drank like a footballer, wasn't squeamish, enjoyed outdoorsy stuff and already got on well with all my friends. Beyond an appreciation of books and songs, we didn't share a particularly deep spiritual or intellectual connection but that didn't trouble me at the time. In pretty short order, we were very much in love, with a bedrock of familiarity beneath it which meant we were genuinely comfortable and kind with one another too.

My female friends from school had visited my house a few times, but normally for parties when their attention lay firmly on the other guests and not the configuration of my household. Once Suzie and I got together, I knew the moment of truth couldn't be deferred for long. The following weekend she stayed at my house and met Mum properly for the first time.

My heart beat painfully when I brought them together. Suzie's natural impulse was to bring light and fun to every interaction, even if she had to fake it, but this time it seemed genuine. She smiled her bright smile and shook Mum's hand, towering above her like a German heroine. Mum's shy friendliness was a neat match for Suzie's, and they hit it off at once. Caro was warm and welcoming too.

I took Suzie upstairs and showed her around, waiting for the inevitable questions about Caro's place in my family. But either she had already gleaned it from Rick or she was too considerate of other people's social discomfort to raise the matter. I decided to broach it myself.

'In case you're wondering, Caro is Mum's girlfriend. I think I told you before, I haven't lived with Dad for a few years.'

'Right. Wicked,' said Suzie, which meant that it was a good arrangement. She didn't skip a beat or raise an eyebrow, and seemed much more interested in the layout of the top floor. 'I didn't know you had a kitchen up here. You're set!'

She took my hand and led me to my room.

21

REiNVENTiON

Over the coming months Suzie and I were inseparable and my studies took a back seat. I spent most of the HSC study period staring out the window and imagining things we could do together, so the exam results, when they came through at the end of the year, were predictably disappointing. I did pretty well by most people's standards (430 in the old measure, which is an ATAR of about 97 nowadays), but well down on my previous results and not enough to get into law at a top-tier university.

You'd think someone who'd spent the last two years going to parties would be inured to the shock of academic underperformance. Not me. I'd somehow deluded myself into believing that I was both an outlaw and a scholar. The world had not bought the first bit (because I still looked like a librarian). But it did buy the second – my family, friends and peers all believed I would cruise into law at Sydney University and waft magisterially into legal practice or a career in academia. Sadly, that bit wasn't true either. It's fair to say the exam results provoked a minor identity crisis. Not only did I have to explain to my father, and others that I was not so special, I also had to reimagine myself as an average Joe.

I'd been accepted into law at Macquarie Uni, where all my friends (including Suzie) were also going. My old friend George and I had already decided to defer university for a year, and my exam results had confirmed that I needed to get my head right before attempting any further study. Average Joes did average work, so I landed a very average job as a 'glassy' at the Epping Hotel. This meant I walked around the pub picking up empty schooners, cleaning out ashtrays and occasionally going downstairs to Tracks Nightclub to do the same. In my mind, I'd made the transition to adulthood – I was earning a real wage and mixing with hard men who drank to excess, gambled, dealt drugs and periodically punched each other to a pulp.

In reality, I was living with my mother who still did all the cooking and cleaning and took care of rent and bills. Moreover, I drove a car that was paid for by my father. As for the hard men of the Epping Hotel, even the tradesmen in the public bar were firmly middle class. My regular weekend shifts usually saw a handful of old blokes drinking shandies and watching the races on the TAB screen. Any drug dealing was confined to a few grams of pot wrapped up in tinfoil, and the occasional fight was typically an 'air swing' from a drunk followed by a cuddle from a bouncer.

My new persona was taking shape nicely. I was a rugged young man, navigating the mean streets of Epping (populated, as they were, by retirees and Chinese accountants). I began supporting the Penrith Panthers, seeing myself in their working-class fan base and 'battler' status. I taught myself the guitar and played riffs from 1970s metal bands on my nylon string acoustic. And I grew my hair until it formed a lank 'bum head'.

The only internal tension I felt at this inauthentic image was the fear of disappointing Dad. While all of the Roberts children seemed happy to embarrass Dad socially, I had a deep need to earn his approval through achievement. I was especially worried that my HSC result had lowered me in his estimation. In fact, he was surprisingly cool about it, and surprisingly cool in general.

Dad had put me in touch with some of his legal friends, all of whom downplayed the significance of my HSC result. They reassured me there were plenty of avenues to legal practice, and qualifications from a second-tier law school were no impediment to success. When I went to dinner with Dad to celebrate the end of school, it was almost as if I'd emerged from the chrysalis state of childhood that had always been so uninteresting to him and I was now one of the initiated.

My father was mellower than I'd ever seen him, and I couldn't attribute that to the wine alone, because he only drank a few glasses. In the dim light of a small restaurant in Potts Point, we faced each other without any of the usual awkwardness or broken eye contact. He subverted my expectations all night, confiding that he'd only ever wanted us to do something that made us happy. Conventional success was never part of his grand design for the children; we'd somehow imposed that on ourselves, maybe by filling the vacuum about career expectations with the image of his own career success. His example had been an intimidating one. I'd set my sights on law, knowing my aversion to sick people ruled me out of medicine, and concluding that a job with a wig was the only one that could come close to matching my father's achievements.

Towards the end of the evening, I coyly raised the subject of homosexuality by describing one of my school friends who'd recently 'come out' and asking if Dad had experienced something similar in his social circle. 'Oh yes,' said Dad. 'The braver ones are honest about it. Jan, I think you've met her. She's a good friend. Some other colleagues never admitted it, but it becomes obvious, you know.' He shrugged as if to say he didn't care either way.

I recalled the times I'd heard him admiringly refer to men as 'handsome', sometimes in reference to war heroes, artists or actors from his youth such as Cary Grant. And he wasn't just open in his appreciation of male beauty – he clearly worried about his own appearance more than the archetypal Aussie bloke. That night, his gold red hair was styled in a neat wave, back and across his forehead, and his navy blazer had a velvety sheen under the soft lights.

I worried that my own appearance was sub-standard and tried to straighten the collar on my shirt. 'I think I'm starting to go bald,' I said, pointing to the mild widow's peak that had become more obvious as I grew my hair. 'You're okay, I think,' he reassured me vaguely. 'There's not much we can do about those things anyway. Good tailoring, that's important. The rest is just … vanity.' He said this less emphatically than it appears on paper; more as if he was musing through the answers himself. I felt a sense of wonder at these new aspects of my father and the access to male wisdom that I was finally gaining after going so long without.

At the end of the night, we hugged goodbye on the street and the love between us was more obvious to me than at any time before. In the following weeks we met many times, usually at the various golf clubs of which he was a member. At The Australian we played a game of tennis. Once again, he appeared relaxed. I was the more nervous one – eager to make a sporting impression. I beat him narrowly and was thrown by his reaction. He was gracious in defeat, praising my serve, and was proud to introduce me to some of his fellow club members afterwards, when he took me to the bar for a single cool beer.

The following week we played snooker at Pennant Hills Golf Club. I entered this contest with much more confidence, having honed my pool game in pubs up and down the northside over the last eighteen months. But I was wrong-footed again when the old man flogged me – effortlessly guiding balls across the ocean of green velvet. 'Longer tables are devilish, aren't they?' he sympathised afterwards.

A strange and marvellous picture was reforming around the man I thought I knew. He could still be gruff and frightening. But he was also wise, disapproving of competitive nonsense, accepting of homosexuality, surprisingly active and moderate in his drinking. Just as startling: he'd clearly misspent his youth in pool halls.

22

AGEiNG

People don't age in a linear fashion. They normally hold the line for years at a time before falling suddenly to a new plateau, where they hold again until the next 'slip'. The year after school was a 'slip' year for me and, weirdly enough, for most of my family too.

Oma's memory problems and paranoia had built to the point that she needed to be moved into a retirement village. Mum managed the process and moved her to a 'village' with support services, just up the road from our place. With the loss of her mind, there was no commensurate decline in worry levels. Some people with dementia are said to move eventually to a state of placid simplicity. Unfortunately, Oma's was either a different breed of dementia or she never made it to that nirvana. She would forget what she had been worrying about but still recall that there had been something to worry about, until all that remained was a generalised sensation of worry with no particulars.

Mum was concerned that she had inherited Oma's gene for dementia, so she read up furiously on the disease and committed herself to a list of preventative measures – exercise, learning new skills, fish oils, etc. – to the point where most of her free time seemed to revolve around learning a new instrument (at first the cello, then the shakuhachi, an obscure Japanese instrument with its own arcane system of notation), setting daily walking targets and eating seafood. Ironically, I could see more of Oma's neurotic tendencies in this obsessional anti-ageing regime than in anything that was evident before the 'treatment' started.

Around 11 p.m. when Caro and Josh were well asleep, I often lay awake in my loft bed with a book, listening to Mum's wobbly exploration of a second-grade cello study. If I ever went down for a glass of milk on those occasions, I would spy Mum in the lounge/music room, her bow making intermittent crunching noises and her left hand moving uncertainly to a spot that was always a fraction from the note. I wondered if the cello's feminine lines played a part in her instrument choice, especially when I saw her wrapped so intently around its 'waist', wearing only her undies in the warmer months.

Mum was a long way from dementia but the first signs of age were creeping up upon her. Now 46 years old, time had left its footprints at the corners of her eyes, despite all the creams and care. Her blue-black hair had faded and thinned to the point that she cut it short and dyed it dark again. And the loss of muscle mass in her back looked like the start of the process that had left Oma so bent and birdlike. After defying gravity for so long, it must have been frightening to head toward Earth, even if Mum still looked fifteen years younger than her age. Any insecurity about losing her beauty must have been heightened by the loss of 'spark' between her and Caro around this time. Without knowing the details, I think they must have stopped having sex regularly.

A trainee school counsellor had fallen for Caro at the school where they worked together. With strong lesbian urges but no example or guide rail to cling to, this young lady had asked Caro about her private life and been happily stunned by the answers. More than just a role model, Caro was soon the object of this woman's affections and, in time, Caro reciprocated. Mum faced the reality of this relationship challenge with her usual bravery and generosity. Never one to let jealousy or convention stop people living a full life, Mum allowed Caro to experiment with a new sexual partner. Mum had her own work colleague expressing interest in her, but unlike Caro, was content with the friendship on offer.

One Saturday I came downstairs for my usual breakfast at noon, to find two strangers with Mum and Caro in the lounge room. One woman was petite, with mousy brown hair. She looked to be in her early thirties.

'Hi, I'm Anita,' she said softly. She seemed shy and sweet.

'And I'm Sharon,' said the other lady in a rich voice. She was grey haired, heavy set and looked like a prison warden, but that impression was entirely undone by her gentle eyes. 'I work with your mum. I've heard a lot about you.' This could have meant anything from violin playing to drunken car crashes, so I left it untouched.

Small talk was an exquisite torture for me at this age. I waited for something witty or perceptive to dance from my synapses, but the wait extended until our guests thought I might have had a stroke. In the end, I muttered goodbye instead of hello and retreated to the kitchen. I consoled myself by thinking I would never see them again, but I was wrong. Anita and Sharon were regular visitors from then on, and it became clear that Anita, at least, was Caro's new lover. Sharon's position was less clear. As far as I could tell, Mum and Caro still regarded themselves as a solid couple, and were still affectionate and supportive with one another. The new player/s had only been recruited to expand their social sphere and enliven the bedroom.

With the increase in foot traffic up our front path, the gate was left open and Caddy the rescue dog was struck by a car when she ran outside. She could drag a child to the side of the pool but she couldn't avoid cars travelling at 60 kilometres an hour. It was a hard lesson in mortality for young Josh, who nursed Caddy in the back of the car all the way to the vet – the little kelpie shivering and bleeding her life away in his lap. He and Caro came home bloodstained and hugging each other for comfort. Joshy was only ten but already taller than Caro and well on his way to being taller than me. His enormous head no longer looked so ridiculous now that the rest of him had caught up. But despite his size, in moments like these I had to remind myself that he was still a boy, and Caro was every bit his parent.

The death of pets always played an uneasy note in the back of my mind, beyond the shock of the event itself, as I'd begun to associate it with harbingers of change. But we didn't need a Roman augur to tell us that Dad was heading for an abrupt change – he'd had about two years of angina to do that for him. His heart specialist confirmed that a bypass was needed and we all saw him in the lead-up to the surgery. I saved my visit for the day of the operation.

The nurses steered me to his private room and I found him reading quietly in bed. He looked as if he was leaching into the white sheets and I imagined this was our last goodbye. After some initial talk about the mechanics of the operation itself, I cut to the chase.

'Dad, I feel like we don't really know each other, or that we're just starting to … get there, you know?'

'It's okay,' he said, patting my hand by the bed rail. But it wasn't okay. He would rather have avoided conversations like this. In fact, he'd have preferred to go under the knife right then in order to escape it. I tried another tack.

'I was angry sometimes, about things, when we were kids …' I breathed the disinfected air and waited for divine inspiration.

'It's all right. It's a routine procedure,' said Dad, the subtext being that we would have plenty of time to avoid these conversations in the future.

I left the room tearful and strangely relieved for such a communication failure.

But something in my appeal must have got through because we both made more of an effort after that. A week or two later, I visited him in his lonely tower. I said 'Shit, Dad!' in shock when he greeted me at the door with his new face and body. The procedure and diet had stripped him of 20 kilos. In retrospect, they probably weren't the words of assurance that a man in recovery needed to hear. And we settled in to order a pizza for dinner, which probably wasn't the food that a man in recovery needed to eat.

Together we watched the sky redden. The afternoon sun was setting early due to smoke from a dozen fires that were destroying the northern suburbs of Sydney. We talked freely, albeit within the safe bounds of literature, history and film. The beauty and horror of events outside the glass took the focus from us and we were strangely at peace.

Back home the next night, Mark came to Beecroft for one of his rare visits, in part to debrief about Dad. Mark had given up alcohol and his appearance had changed almost as much as Dad's. An overload of cocaine in the heady days of sound engineering for Jimmy Barnes and Noiseworks (when drugs and girls were inexhaustible, and he had the looks and money to capitalise on both) had left him with very little hair. He was still handsome, but now he'd lost that florid/swollen look of the drunk, I could see he was very much his mother's son – all elfin features and delicate bones.

Upstairs on my balcony, Mark told me he'd taken up meditation. He'd attended a Buddhist retreat in the Blue Mountains where he'd been encouraged to dig up things from our childhood.

'How did you feel about Mum leaving Dad, back at the old house?' I asked him, keen to hear his thoughts on Mum and Caro.

He took a drag on his cigarette and looked out across our leaf-strewn pool. 'I was glad for you guys.'

I hadn't expected him to take that line. It sounded like he would have been happy to live with Mum and Caro if that'd been on offer when he was my age.

'Did you blame anyone?' I asked. 'I mean, for tension at home.'

He shrugged and stubbed out his cigarette.

'Mum was young and still trying to work things out. Dad was under pressure. It must have been hard for them too.' Matter-of-fact and gracious, the new sober Mark was a revelation.

I was changing too. Unlike most of my friends, I continued to grow after school and while I would never be tall, rounding out at about 5 foot 11, I was no longer short. I also put on a little weight, which congregated mostly around my face and stomach, courtesy of a 'beer and burgers' diet. My hair faded from white blond to more of a fishpond yellow. And my brain took a substantial hit from my new pastime – smoking marijuana.

I'd first smoked pot with Rick when we were about thirteen. I think we got it from my neighbour, who was an older and much cooler kid. We sat in a crude picnic shelter in the park behind my house and, with one toke of a joint, rode a sharp spike from normal to high and back again. It inspired Rick to experiment with a high voice. We must have laughed for half an hour as he spoke nonsense in castrati tones – sort of shy at the spectacle he was making of himself but too happy to care.

From then on, pot was a prized commodity but it was hard to obtain. Occasionally we got lucky with local tough guys, combining our $5 and $10 bills for pathetic seed-ridden spoils. Sometimes we travelled 50 minutes by train to Kings Cross, where Nate, always the boldest of us, bought $20 sticks from dealers in pool halls.

The whole mood of the night hinged precariously on that one transaction. Score and everything was jubilant. But fail to get on or worse, get ripped off, and we'd all ride the train home in silence, Nate holding the doors open and spitting to wring some small mischief from the adventure. Looking at photos of us from this time, baby cheeks, foal-like bodies, it's laughable to think we ever scored and even funnier to think how outraged we'd get when it didn't come off.

Places we could safely smoke were limited and usually

involved industrial spaces like tunnels under stations, or suburban bushland, small, sheltered clearings by stagnant creeks, wrappers and rubbish lying about. We became innovators with smoking utensils: papers if they were available (that would end up spit sodden and mangled), pin holes in Coke cans (the pot resting on top), pipes fashioned from tubes and Blu Tack, cones made from the foil that the pot came in.

Pot rituals were a little less feral in our later teens, probably due to the influence of the girls who started showing up at our parties, but it was still done on the sly. Only when we left school did it become a regular fixture, with some of my friends spending the better part of their university lives stoned or asleep. Don was the first of our group to move out of home, so his place became the natural focal point for nineteen-year-olds intent on mischief.

Don rented a tiny loft above a carport in Epping. The roof was so low you had to walk with a hunch and you could feel the heat from the light bulb in the ceiling. For a nominal sum, Don was given the run of this dollhouse, where he, Sidney (a Northern Beaches boy who'd boarded at the college) and I punched through dozens of cones. The landlord was a gay octogenarian called Ron, who occasionally fed us dinner in the main house and told us stories about the Arabs who'd propositioned him in the Middle East during World War II.

The poor old guy was lonely and afraid of his other tenant – an Iranian man who pissed in the shower. Having Don around provided a bit of sexual frisson to a fading life. I remember sitting in that darkened lounge room, heavy with antiques, listening to Ron's quaint but directionless stories. His thin voice emerged uncertainly from behind the cravat he always wore to disguise his chicken-skin neck. We impolitely shovelled down our food and raced back up to the loft for more cones. He no doubt heard the three of us giggling at all hours of the night and figured we were on his team.

Pot was no longer a fun, frivolous thing; it was becoming more profound. Smoking in those days involved listening intently to music, a lot of it cheesy 1970s schlock like The Eagles and Queen, and marvelling at the way the drug could remove all preconceptions that tainted the listening process. Stripped of associations, like the kind of people who liked The Eagles, one could apply virgin ears. There was also an autistic kind of focus that came with pot, which might have made conversation difficult but allowed the listener to zero in on a particular instrument and follow its journey with child-like wonder.

Our nightly smoking marathons often ended with a kebab from the service station on the corner of Epping Road. It was here, after one of the more embarrassing moments of my life, that I decided marijuana was becoming a problem. The three of us entered the service station shop around midnight. The whole room glowed brighter than a spaceship and I felt as if I'd been caught shoplifting, quite certain that all eyes in the store were upon me.

Don and Sidney chose their snacks from the shelves but I

was transfixed by the Hot Chicken Hero in the display cabinet. I tried to open the cabinet but it was very stiff. I had to use more and more force, until the thing finally released with a loud crack. I looked around to see if anyone was staring, then took the food to the microwave for heating, feeling uncertain but trying valiant self-talk – 'Marijuana can induce paranoia, you've done nothing wrong.' After two minutes of cooking, I took the package to the counter to make my purchase, amazed at the weightlessness of the thing. In an attempt to be an assertive consumer, I said to the attendant, 'You don't get much for your money these days.'

He frowned, took the package from me, then shook his head in wonder.

'Where did you get this from, mate?' he asked.

I pointed to the cabinet.

'That's the display cabinet,' he explained. 'Which you've just broken, by the way. You've heated up some newspaper inside that package. The food's in the fridge,' He pointed in the right direction.

'You know,' he went on, still genuinely in wonder, 'We get all sorts of people in here, from the pub and stuff – pissheads, smackies. But you are the dumbest cunt I've ever seen.'

I nodded in agreement. The two people behind me in the queue were laughing, and I went straight out without a word.

Towards the end of that year, things had begun to shift away from the innocent idyll we three had enjoyed. Don failed some of his uni subjects and Sidney failed all of them.

Don had to study harder and poor Sidney got a job packing shelves at Coles. Years later, Sidney earned multiple degrees but at the time he was raging against his shit life and started using his ready wit to belittle and destabilise us. Fractures were beginning to show in our friendship – alliances, real and imagined, forming between two of us at the expense of the other and then realigning again.

Then Don began to develop marijuana-induced psychosis, explaining to me one night, with his eyes squirming about the room, that he was going mad and could never smoke pot again. I think his Latvian heritage inured him to many things, including alcohol poisoning and cold weather, but pot was not part of the Arctic genetic coding and he would have been institutionalised if he'd kept going. Wisely returning to beer and dropping the accountancy part of his course, he got back on track within a few months.

While I wasn't going nuts from smoking pot, it wasn't doing me much good either. The first hour or so after a 'hit' was characterised by a racing heart and an edgy sensation bordering on panic. When that phase wore off, I'd settle into a slugged-out lobotomy where thoughts moved at half-speed and I could demolish a family-sized pizza on my own. Friends noted that I was less entertaining these days, and Mum was worried enough to take me aside and say, 'When you chip bits off your brain, Tobes, you can't get them back.'

She must have been saddened by the decline in her golden boy, who only a few years earlier had been fresh faced, precocious and on track for academic glory. Now I was a lank-haired stoner who liked watching rugby league. Thankfully, I'd saved enough money from my shifts at the pub to take a big overseas holiday with George, just as we'd planned the year before. I think everyone hoped the new experiences might impart some much-needed life skills and maybe reignite some intellectual curiosity before my brain got too stuck in a parochial bog.

As the departure date approached, I found myself getting quite nervous. Not only was I very comfortable at home having everything done for me, but Suzie was a delight in this early phase of our relationship and I could hardly imagine life without her now. I was also worried about Mum and Caro. It was clear that Caro and her new friend Anita were becoming more serious, and while Mum would never stop a partner from exploring boundaries, I could see that she was feeling hurt and unsettled. I wasn't sure if I would come home to a girlfriend who still loved me or parents who were still together.

The few weeks before I flew out of Sydney, I'd actually seen Mum and Caro wrestling in the music room. They'd grappled playfully in the past but this time it was different. When I came in, Caro had a dominant hold, gripping Mum around the waist and bearing her to the floor. They had smiles on their faces, which initially stopped me from feeling too alarmed. But on closer inspection, the smiles were fixed in a joyless rictus, and they were both panting hard enough to suggest that this tussle was being fought in earnest.

Mum was giving away at least 20 kilos in the contest, so she had to make do with speed and guile. As Caro went to press her advantage, Mum surprised her by ceasing to resist, dropping the remaining inches to the floor and slipping back between Caro's arms. The move showed some genuine ring craft, and Mum pulled it off like a striking snake. Caro was left with only a partial hold on Mum's shoulder and head. Her strong arms began to squeeze the most from that partial grasp, but Mum had enough space now to insert her legs and kick herself free with a grunt. They reset and turned to face each other on their knees – Caro implacably planted on the floor, Mum's steely wrists reaching for a new hold, her sinews and blue veins more apparent than ever.

I knocked on the door frame to prevent them from going on with it. 'You know they have jelly for fights like this at Penrith Panthers,' I said, trying to change the atmosphere. They both stood up and laughed to conceal the intensity of what I'd just witnessed.

Later that night I tried to explain the scene to Suzie.

'Were they serious or kidding around?' she asked, a little worried.

'I dunno. A bit of both, I think?'

Among other things, a bust up between Mum and Caro had the potential to completely unstitch Josh. He'd just put a drawing on the fridge which showed a little cottage with smoke coming out of the chimney and the words 'I love God, Mummy and Caro' written in texta underneath.

Those fears aside, everyone agreed that I needed a jolt of something new. Well I'm ashamed to say that the trip didn't really shock me out of any bad habits – George and I did pretty much the same things overseas that we'd been doing back home. But at least we saw that foreigners got pissed and took drugs in slightly different ways.

23

TRAVEL

Our first stop was Los Angeles and I was overwhelmed from the start. Everything was amplified, like an apocalyptic glimpse of Sydney's future. Traffic was noisier, people shouted at each other for no reason, food was fattier and sweeter, cigarettes were so strong they made my hands shake, advertising billboards stood taller by the roadside, and the quality of light was even starker than an Australian summer.

Within minutes of touching down we were hurtling along a freeway in a hostel bus with no seat belts. We sloshed around in the back like spilt beer. To calm our nerves, we took ourselves to the nearest bar for Budweiser and straight whisky shots, where we met a diminutive Latino called Rahul who looked like he had intestinal worms. For some reason, Rahul took a shine to us.

He led us across the city towards his place in downtown LA. When we stopped by a busy roadside, I heard a high-pitched cracking sound and wondered at the sudden movement of people. Rahul urged us to run with everyone else and it wasn't until I was crouching around the corner that I realised we were in the middle of a shootout. Car tyres squealed out on the road and a man in a tracksuit sprinted past our hiding spot and jumped a world-record height to clear the wire fence behind us. It was still full daylight.

Minutes later the crowds returned and life resumed as normal. Our new friend assured us it was fine to continue up the street but I insisted he find an alternative route where men in tracksuits didn't shoot each other. Back at Rahul's house, we talked books and it became clear he was an unpublished author, with all the bitterness and self-loathing that entails. He was self-conscious about the state of his little apartment and apologised in between sullen rants about trying to do something for travellers. I think he may have imagined his apartment and himself through our judging eyes – a loser in a dingy dive. In reality, we didn't think twice about his apartment. It was better than my room back home. We just thought he was becoming odd. Two beers later he smashed a bottle against the wall and shouted, 'All I care about is books.' Beer ran slowly over the books on the floor.

George suggested to our host that if things were going to get violent it was unlikely to end well for him, given that he was a short scribe and George was a 14-stone footballer, though I think the actual words were something like, 'That was weird. Don't make me hit you.' I was still wondering how smashing a full bottle of beer against the wall was going to help with the man's house-pride issues.

'What?' He asked George to repeat himself. There was a long silence in which our (by now very drunk) host forgot his own question and the incident which had sparked it. He rolled a joint for us to smoke and insisted that Joseph Conrad was not really one of the greats. Knowing the frustrations of the literary world as I do now, his behaviour makes perfect sense to me, but at the time I was quite confused.

'Let's get out of this dump,' he said and took us to a club down the street. I don't know what the joint contained but it kicked in strongly at the club, which was lit to highlight certain frequencies such as lipstick. Beautiful but faintly ghastly Latino women talked to us through electric mouths that seemed to move independently of their shadowy faces.

Our Mexican friend said the chicks were going to love us and then went to the toilet. We took that moment to run away from him and the club, quite certain by that stage that he was a lunatic. Out on the street, my impaired memory reverted to Sydney road rules and George had to save me from being run over on several occasions by jerking me back from oncoming cars. We set off on our dangerous walk home, across LA in the middle of the night, and made it back to the hostel just as dawn began to stain the surrounding freeway coils.

You'd think that experience would have discouraged us from getting smashed in a foreign place but it didn't. In fact, the next few months were a blur of drunken mistakes, failed scores, robberies, motorbike accidents and other near-death experiences. On one occasion, George went into a basement in Rome to complete a drug transaction and when he failed to emerge several hours later, I began rehearsing the telephone conversation I would have to have with his parents – 'I'm sorry Mrs Weaver, your son seems to have been kidnapped or murdered. It's just one of those terribly unlucky things that can happen when you try to buy drugs from Italian gangsters. We took every precaution.'

George returned looking badly shaken. They'd taken his money, given him some tissues with nothing in them and threatened to kill him when he complained. The whole episode was terrifying enough to make me call my mother that night, just to hear the sounds of home again. Caro answered the phone. I was surprised at the warm feeling of comfort that I derived from her voice, even delayed and echoing across the Indian Ocean.

'Toby! Your mum will be thrilled to speak to you. She's been missing you so terribly that she has started carrying a pair of your old socks around with her.'

'That's weird,' I said. And it was, though touching too.

'I'll get your mum.' Caro put the phone down. The word 'honey' reverberated through the halls of my darkened home in Beecroft.

A few seconds later, Mum came on the line sounding almost apologetic. 'Hello?'

'Hi Mum.'

'Oh, darling – it's so wonderful to hear your voice. Where are you?'

'We're in Rome.'

'You sound ... subdued. Are you all right?'

'Yeah. Just feeling a bit homesick I think ... we got robbed today.'

'Really? How?'

'Just buying some things.' This was technically true.

'That happens in Rome. Are you being careful?'

'Absolutely.' I said this last bit with conviction, knowing that we'd only ever approached people who looked like they could actually provide the drugs we wanted.

Mum gave me the latest news on Ren, Josh and the others, before explaining that Annie had to be put down. For a moment, my clouded mind thought that was Caro's new girlfriend and it seemed quite an extreme response to a love rival, then Mum explained that our old Alsatian had cancer and we had to let her go. I felt faintly unnerved by a memory of pets long dead and everything they seemed to presage.

The touch of home was enough to recharge me for another few weeks, but it wasn't long before things went awry again. This time it was enough to make me reconsider the whole thing. We were staying in a youth hostel in Crete, which meant sharing a room with a bunch of dreadlocked hippies.

Even the hostel owners apologised about the quality of our bunkmates. They drank some kind of intoxicant from jars, played bongos out of time and chanted nonsense.

The next day, a large Dutchman joined the group room and, seeming refreshingly sane, George and I formed an alliance with him. Drinking in a local bar with him that night, he told us interesting facts about life as a Dutch schoolteacher while we warned him about the dickheads with whom he'd be sharing his room that night.

Unfortunately, we must have overstated the nuisance factor or overestimated our Dutch friend's sanity, because as soon as we got back to our room, he immediately stopped the jam session and forcibly removed one man's drum. A hippie on the top bunk began protesting. Our friend then drew a hunting knife, pressed it to the man's throat and issued a series of heavily accented commands, finishing with a last directive 'and don't stink'.

It was this last bit that gave George and I the most amusement the next day, although at the time I have to say I was shitting myself – and in fact we concluded that our hippie roommate must have done the same. That afternoon we met our Dutch friend again for a New Year's Eve drink. Out on the streets of Heraklion in the early evening, I was caught up in one of the strangest New Year's Eves of my life. Every inch of public space was occupied by people exuberantly belting each other with plastic clubs and spraying each other with shaving cream. Particularly vicious clubbings were reserved for young women and were generally meted out by men in packs. Looking down the street, clubs rose and fell like a choppy sea.

Bewilderment turned to fear when I was set upon by a gang of youths and I found that the plastic clubs were surprisingly hard. I threw a punch to defend myself, which resulted in a full-on brawl. When I finally disentangled myself and shouted 'Piss off' at the locals, it became clear that people didn't normally object to these lighthearted assaults. I had offended them by not playing the game properly.

'I will fight you,' one of my assailants called back to me, as his companions pulled him on down the street to their next quarry. 'Well what were you doing before? Fuckwit,' I muttered, wiping shaving cream from my hair and blood from my nose. There was some profound cross-cultural confusion at work. My teenage years in Australia had taught me that bludgeoning a man repeatedly with a club was a natural way to start a fight. Not so in Crete.

I found George and our big Dutch mate to protect me, but the crowd diminished until there were only a few stubborn groups still whacking away. And by 11 p.m., when I'd expected things to really explode, the streets were empty. At midnight there was just a handful of drunk foreigners to celebrate.

The next morning, feeling bruised and disappointed, I decided it was time to head home. In between blurry sightings of statues and paintings, I'd fallen off scooters, been punched in the face, lost money to strangers and vomited in toilets all over Europe. I'd ridden my luck very hard and got the sense that a more permanent mishap was just around the corner if I didn't sober up.

By late January 1991 I was happily settled back in Beecroft, and preparing to start the next phase of life with renewed focus – university.

24

MUM'S TRIALS

Suzie and I were ecstatic to be together again. We both attended Macquarie Uni, sometimes even sharing lectures, meaning we were inseparable that year. We shared my little car and she stayed at Beecroft most of the time. There was an effortless ease about our relationship at this time, and both our sets of friends got on beautifully.

While alcohol was still a feature of our lives together (it was impossible to avoid that culture within our circle of friends), I'd sworn off pot, and we were too active now to afford profound hangovers. Most weekends we played tennis, in summer we went camping, in winter we drove to the snow. We also pushed each other at uni and I studied hard for the first time in years. As a result, I did well across the board, earning high grades in law and English, and even getting a letter from the statistics department asking if I'd considered a career in maths (I hadn't).

The relationship between Mum and Suzie was another

bonus. Both shy, averse to conflict, natural peacekeepers, they also loved the arts, so they'd hit it off easily the year before. With more time together, that mutual regard had blossomed into adoration. I almost felt excluded when they settled into their marathon chats at the kitchen table.

Suzie was comfortable with Mum's sexuality from the start. She was also very protective of her. Among other things, Suzie urged me to be more demonstrative and caring with Mum – she knew the depth of love there, but pressed me to show it.

The relationship between Caro and Suzie was not quite as comfortable. A bit like Ren, Suzie was able to stage a masterful performance, pushing through awkward silences with the obligatory laughs and small talk that I could never manage. Caro was always polite towards her, but I think she saw Suzie as part of the wider problem – that is, one of the 'enablers' who allowed me to shirk adulthood and live like a princeling at home. In particular, Suzie was a good cook who loved being able to give something back to the household by conjuring up spicy Asian dishes. And I loved being able to take something away from the household by eating them. To Caro's eyes, this looked like an extension of the spoilt nonsense I'd got away with for years under Mum.

The growing tension between Caro and Mum may have also contributed to the stilted interactions with Suzie. We all knew something wasn't right. Caro was spending more time with Anita, and there was a seriousness or even sadness to Mum now, especially in her discussions with Caro. Years later,

Mum told me that during this period with Caro the situation had become increasingly unfair and she'd asked Caro to clarify the status of their relationship.

In the middle of those delicate negotiations, things got even tougher for Mum when Oma's health deteriorated. She'd caught a virus in the nursing home and a nasty cough quickly morphed into pneumonia. She seemed to recover, at least physically, within a few weeks. We only learnt later that the illness had put some strain on her heart. Somehow the impact on her body also pushed her dementia into a whole new category of disorientation.

We all knew Oma was fading and it suddenly occurred to me that my window for having a lucid conversation with her would soon be closed. On a Saturday afternoon I walked the two blocks to her retirement village, feeling ashamed for not having done it more often. Mum visited Oma at least once a fortnight, whereas I'd done it once in two years.

The gardens were beautiful but the building was tired, and the wing where residents received nursing care felt too similar to a hospital to be homely. The linoleum on the floor was lifting in bubbles and the smell of disinfectant blended with the scent of aged flesh. Oma and her fellow residents were seated in recliner chairs pushed back to the walls of the common room. A nurse with a slightly forced attitude of positivity took me to my grandmother's side and said very loudly, 'Irene. You have a visitor!'

'Hello,' said Oma with an uncertain smile.

'Hi Oma. It's me, Toby.'

'Oh, hello,' she said, her smile broadening enough to suggest we were making progress.

'Are you feeling better?' I asked.

'Hmm? I think so …' she said, as if it depended on your point of comparison.

'Mum's coming to see you tomorrow,' I offered, in the hope that this might get a more enthusiastic response.

'Oh, all right,' she said, clearly wondering why a stranger would need to bring their mum as well.

'Your daughter,' I clarified.

'Oh, you know her!' she said, and her whole demeanor changed. She was alive again.

'Yeah, that's Mum.'

'Isn't she an angel,' she said, squeezing my hand.

I nodded and patted the papery skin on her fingers.

We sat quietly for a few minutes more, until her smile began to fade. Then I said goodbye and walked home, fighting tears.

Not long after that, Oma died of heart failure. I took some comfort from Mum's description of her in death. Apparently her face relaxed for the first time in decades, and looked much younger, finally free of the concerns that so dogged her in life. Mum was heartbroken; more heartbroken than I'd expected. Knowing how sick Oma had been in the preceding years, and seeing how annoying she could be with her incessant telephone calls, it was easy to forget the strength of the bond between mother and child. Oma was still Mum's mum, and now she was gone I think Mum felt a flood of guilt for all the times she'd left the phone off the hook.

A series of waves were crashing over Mum – Oma's death, a growing sense of her own mortality, and the prospect of losing her partner to a younger lover. My sister dropped in on her one afternoon to see how she was coping. Ren found her curled on the bed, howling in despair. When Ren had calmed her down enough to talk, Mum confided that a terrible darkness seemed to have enveloped her and the only thing that kept her anchored to the world now was a sense of duty to her children.

Ren was still feeling shaken when she debriefed with me the next day. Mum was always more willing to be vulnerable with Ren. Around me, she strove to stay in control, and I'm glad of it, because I wouldn't have coped seeing Mum so unhinged. But even Josh and I could tell that she was struggling. It was a full month before she was laughing again.

25

A FRESH START

The start of summer signalled a series of new beginnings for my family. First, Mum bought a dog. As my first year at university drew to a close, I came home to find a gangly Doberman crashing through the flower beds. 'This is Bella,' Mum announced proudly. There was a look of fear in the dog's eyes. And it had every right to be afraid. I think Annie was the only one of our dogs who'd died from natural causes, so maybe Bella could sense that she'd landed with a family tainted by criminal neglect.

Bella quickly grew to the normal size associated with that breed, though she never developed a Doberman's knack for taking instruction. We called her 'the thinker'. She drank saltwater from the pool and ate splinters of wood. She also ate bees and wondered at the painful swelling that followed. Carrying large things in her mouth was her only trick and we praised her for that, if only to discourage bee eating. In addition to being mentally defective, a dog psychologist would no doubt have diagnosed some kind of personality disorder in Bella, which manifested itself in frantic leaping when visitors arrived.

The joy of watching a puppy engage with the world must have been the perfect circuit-breaker for Mum – opening her own eyes to new possibilities around her. A young lady at work complimented Mum on her sense of style and Mum was so embarrassed she blushed. A few coffee dates later and Mum was already imagining a better life, away from the complications that had sprung up around Caro. By the end of summer, Mum and her new friend Jenny were very tight, and Mum had begun the difficult process of breaking up with Caro.

To hear Mum tell it now, it was the affair with Anita, and the ongoing tension between Caro and me, which ultimately brought them unstuck. Those things aside, there was still an enormous amount of love between them, so the separation was very painful for them both. I got the sense that, of the two, Caro was more hurt by the process, which is interesting given she was still seeing Anita.

Mum was no doubt distracted from the pain of separation by the growing love between her and Jenny. I met Jenny at our house shortly before the start of my second year at uni. Much shyer than Caro, she came wanting to fit in. Jenny was short and powerfully built, like Caro, though her short-back-and-sides haircut, coupled with a sharp suit, made her look androgynous or even boyish. She had large brown eyes and spoke quickly, perhaps from nerves. We got on well from the start.

Just as we were all adjusting to these seismic shifts at home, my father introduced us to the new love in his life – a middle-aged divorcee called Lene. Now in his early fifties, Dad's taste in women had evolved. For a time, he'd led a double life in Potts Point – by day, a bastion of the conservative medical world; by night, someone who loved rubbing padded shoulders with the colourful denizens of clubs like Rogues in Kings Cross. I think the racy gangster lass we'd met in Avalon a few years earlier had been a product of that world.

Next in line had been Mary, a bookish nerd who shared nothing in common with her predecessor apart from a slight air of superiority and a disdain for children. Dad made a few attempts to introduce Mary to the wider family but no one's heart was in it. With Lene, it was different. We could all see that Dad was really in love this time and Lene made a big effort to engage with all of us.

She had children of her own and we met the whole gang in Dad's penthouse apartment that summer. Lene was petite and aristocratic, with an accent stranded somewhere between Denmark, where she'd grown up, and Oxford, where she'd settled with her first husband. She shook our hands firmly and introduced each of us to her daughter and sons, who seemed very gracious, well-bred and slightly shell-shocked.

Within a few months, Dad had proposed to Lene, declaring her first husband a madman for having let her go. Lene accepted and moved to Sydney. The decision was a good one – the marriage endured and Dad never looked back.

The opening stanza of youth was over and I was confident that all the Roberts clan had found their way through. University life seemed to suit me, and Ren would join me there a year later. Marko was sober. Joshy had just been accepted into James Ruse High School, the most prestigious academic school in the country. Mum and Dad were happily settled with their new partners. There were more trials for all of us in the years ahead but, for the moment, our unconventional family had triumphed.

26

REFLECTiONS

With the gay marriage plebiscite carried so convincingly in 2017, and the large number of openly gay people in positions of influence now, it's easy to forget that life for the gay community was still very tough only a few decades ago. Friends of mine who 'came out' in the 1990s had to think long and hard about how to break it to their loved ones. And in some cases, they chose to leave their old friends behind, or even move overseas to start entirely new lives, rather than try to find acceptance within their old circle.

When I think of the difficult choices made by Mum and the unflinching way she 'owned' those choices, I'm quite amazed at her bravery. In ultra-conservative, blue ribbon Beecroft, she and Caro carried on their life together without a hint of apology or discomfort. And to be fair to the local community, they generally responded to that honesty by accepting the lesbian couple into their neighbourhood. There must have been snide comments and judgmental gossip among some of our neighbours, but I never heard it and I never felt like Mum was being judged.

At school, on the other hand, homosexuality was still regarded as weak or weird by the 'blokier' teachers and students. I did feel Mum being judged on occasion, during parent–teacher interviews for instance, though usually more in relation to her feminism than her homosexuality.

I wish I'd been as brave as Mum when it came to her sexuality. I cringe when I think of all the times I avoided discussing it with friends and peers. While I never felt any personal unease about Mum being gay, I was terrified about the perception of others. I can only say that people nearly always surprised me by accepting Mum wholeheartedly, which is doubly humiliating because it shows I sold both Mum and my peers quite short. Everyone came out of it looking more generous than me.

I'm certain that Mum's nature made the journey of acceptance easier for others to take. And by that I mean even homophobic people would have made an exception in Mum's case, and taken her to their bosom, simply because she is kind to just about everyone she meets. There's no hint of defensiveness or judgment in her conduct, and that tends to bring out the best in others.

Despite my new appreciation of Mum's courage, I shouldn't make too big a deal of it because I never got the sense that she was trying to issue a challenge or champion a cause. In fact, her main focus was on us kids. In many respects she was just a regular suburban mum. Throughout any turmoil in her private life, whether it be the break-up with Dad or the later one with Caro, she remained a consistent, loving force in our lives. And she still is today. I see her or speak to her most weeks, and I know Josh, Ren and Mark enjoy a similarly close bond.

Mum has been with Jenny for 25 years. Like all long-term couples they've had their difficult times, and the age gap presents some challenges (especially now Mum is retired), but they're very good together. Mum is still vivacious and keeps up a punishing regime of dance classes, poetry group, music lessons, art and travel. Jenny clearly adores her and is ferociously protective.

My relationship with Jenny has remained strong. I'm not sure why it has been easier between the two of us than it was between me and Caro. It probably helped that we were closer in age and I was preparing to leave home when we met. In other words, it was almost a relationship of equality and independence from the outset. This may have been the secret to Ren and Caro's easier rapport too.

Josh, on the other hand, struggled with Jenny in the early years. As a reclusive teenager, he had real difficulties connecting with her, and they often clashed over chores, especially where Jenny believed him to be taking advantage of Mum's selflessness. I was not close enough to these problems to diagnose them with any confidence, given I'd moved out of home by this time, but it looked from afar like an eerily similar dynamic to the one that had choked me and Caro.

There are many things about my teen years that haunt me, but my behaviour towards Caro is right up among the most shameful on the list. There are no real excuses for it, but I see now that it stemmed from immaturity, stubbornness and a profound kind of insecurity which meant I was very threatened by a strong female presence in the house. The damage done in those years precluded any chance of a meaningful relationship between the two of us and we have very little contact today.

We see each other once every few years, and those reunions are free of tension, if not free of history. I feel as I would towards a distant cousin – someone I wish well but know so little about now that I can't populate those wishes with anything specific. She seems smaller to me somehow and friendly, which she may have been all along, so I find it very hard to conjure up the threat that she used to represent.

Caro went on to find love again and is happily settled. She and Mum handled their break-up with enviable maturity and stayed firm friends throughout. To this day, they meet for weekly catch-ups and it's clear there is still a lot of love between them, albeit of the platonic kind. Caro also stayed close to Josh. She really was a second mum to him and he still regards her that way. At Josh's place the other day, I saw a card on the dressing room table. It was a note from Caro wishing him a speedy recovery from illness and inviting him on holidays. I felt heartened to see that bond was still strong, and a little ashamed that I hadn't done more to create something as positive and enduring.

'How did our unconventional upbringing affect us?' people may ask. In Josh's case the answer is clear. He's grown into a fine man. Even when I look at old photos, it's tough to recall the anger I used to feel towards him, because not only do we love each other now in a completely unreserved and uncomplicated way, but I can see nothing of the monster that I fought. The photographic record only shows a goofy kid with adorable cheeks, looking sideways up at the camera. He finally grew into that enormous frame, ending up 6 foot 4 and handsome, after years of being mistaken for a dopey kid five years older than he was. Physicality aside, he's also a gentle family man who has devoted his professional life to helping disadvantaged kids.

Mark and I both had the wobbles at various times in our twenties and thirties, but for anyone looking to sheet that home to Mum's choices or choosing to see my dissolute childhood as evidence of the harm that minors suffer when raised by lesbians, the facts don't really support you. Josh was the only one of us who was raised by lesbians from start to finish (having spent so little time around Dad), and he turned out the most abstemious and calm of the bunch. He has the occasional glass of wine, has never been interested in drugs, and is essentially conservative (albeit accepting of difference in all its many forms).

Ren is a close second in the sanity stakes, being a very grounded and wise soul, but the conventional 'family values' narrative would have us believe that she stood to lose the most from having a lesbian mum as a role model. While Ren is joyously comfortable in the company of her lesbian friends and colleagues, she turned out entirely heterosexual and is happily married with a son (not that it would have mattered to her, or us, if she'd turned out lesbian, single and barren).

But this still begs the question – what troubled Mark and me so much that we had to drink like Russian Cossacks? It was probably a mix of things, including some addiction in the family tree, boys trying to emulate their father, a culture in private schools which celebrated drinking, and some social anxieties which were softened by the effects of alcohol. Despite all that, Mark and I managed to bumble through the maze of life, each of us ignoring psychological baggage, self-medicating and hiding for years before emerging unsteadily into adulthood. We stand now, a little odd and unmistakably marked by our early lives, but men with careers, partners, full lives and our essential humanity intact.

Dad has mellowed with age. He still has the occasional outburst but nothing that can't be repaired. I've been able to air the things about our childhood that hurt me and he understands my point of view even if he doesn't always agree with it. And that's good enough for me. We are friends now and share a real bond over books, music and travel. In fact, for two such different temperaments, we have strikingly similar passions.

For those who want to know what became of my friends, I stayed close to Rick and he's still fond of Mum, who he sees once or twice a year at family gatherings. He's a very involved family man himself.

I drifted apart from Nate but we exchange messages every once in a while. When he got out of jail, he got his ticket as an electrician and developed a specialty in wiring mines. He divides his time between dark holes in Western Australia and his new home in Chiang Mai, where he lives with his Thai wife.

Don went on to graduate from economics and become a stockbroker, with his sanity intact. I still play sport with him and we go away together sometimes, in a vain effort to recapture our youth. George remains a wonderful, protective friend. He no longer rescues me from violent strangers but I know he could still do it, because he practises choking people out in wrestling tournaments. Sidney, our old pot-smoking companion, took his hard-earned money from Coles and flew to live in a squat in Berlin. Living with genuine druggies must have sobered him up because he came home, reenrolled in uni and went on to become a senior public servant.

It's something of a cliché to say that children just need love and the shape of the family that provides it is largely irrelevant. But in my case it was true. I felt loved by my parents, their partners, my siblings and my friends. If anything, I had a wider circle of support to draw upon than the average kid.

Some of that was dumb luck and some was good judgment on the part of my parents, who ultimately picked long-term partners who had the best interests of me and my siblings at heart. A good illustration of that point is the way they all rallied around me when I got quite sick, a few years after the events of this book. Ren, Mum, Jenny, Dad and Lene were so good to me through that dark period, it's fair to say I wouldn't have recovered without them.

On balance, I feel fortunate to have had a childhood that exposed me to different ways of living. Once I'd shaken the unease of having a family that was a bit odd, I could appreciate all the wonderful things that came with it: creativity, unstructured fun and a disregard for the rules. Perhaps, most importantly of all, it made me a more empathetic person, knowing, as I do now, how hard it could be for lesbians like Mum to live through that time when mainstream Australia was still struggling to come to terms with their relationships and their role as parents. I can say from first-hand experience that they make pretty good ones.

Other great books from Bad Apple Press

Borderline
ISBN:9780648780779
www.badapplepress.com.au

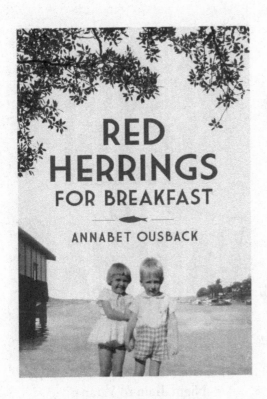

Red Herrings for Breakfast
ISBN:97806485566923
www.badapplepress.com.au

'A jewel of a book' Steve Biddulph

NIGHT TRAIN to VARANASI

India with my daughter

SEAN DOYLE

Night Train to Varanasi
ISBN:9780648556954
www.badapplepress.com.au

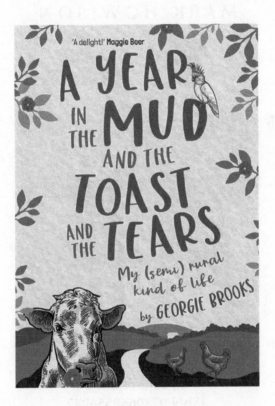

A Year in the Mud and the Toast and
the Tears
ISBN:9780648556916
www.badapplepress.com.au

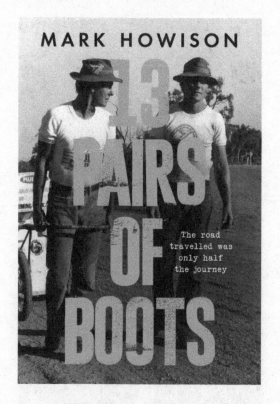

MARK HOWISON

13 PAIRS OF BOOTS

The road
travelled was
only half
the journey

13 Pairs of Boots
ISBN:9780648556947
www.badapplepress.com.au